Collins

T0337296

COBUILD
Key Words for
Automotive
Engineering

HarperCollins Publishers
Westerhill Road
Bishopbriggs
Glasgow
G64 2QT

First Edition 2013

Reprint 10 9 8 7 6 5 4 3 2 1 0

© HarperCollins Publishers 2013

ISBN 978-0-00-748980-0

Collins® and COBUILD® are
registered trademarks of
HarperCollins Publishers Limited

www.collinselt.com and
www.collinsdictionary.com/cobuild

A catalogue record for this book is
available from the British Library

Audio recorded Networks SRL,
Milan, Italy

Acknowledgements
We would like to thank those authors
and publishers who kindly gave
permission for copyright material
to be used in the Collins Corpus.
We would also like to thank Times
Newspapers Ltd for providing
valuable data.

Contents

Contributors

Specialist consultant
Don Goodsell, founding editor of the *Journal of Automotive Engineering*, author of the *Dictionary of Automotive Engineering*, formerly European Acquisitions Editor for the Society of Automotive Engineers

Project manager
Patrick White

Editors
Katherine Carroll
Gavin Gray
Kate Mohideen
Ruth O'Donovan
Enid Pearsons
Elizabeth Walter
Kate Woodford

Computing support
Mark Taylor

For the publisher
Gerry Breslin
Lucy Cooper
Kerry Ferguson
Elaine Higgleton
Rosie Pearce
Lisa Sutherland

Introduction

Collins COBUILD Key Words for Automotive Engineering is a brand-new vocabulary book for students who want to master the English of Automotive Engineering in order to study or work in the field. This title contains the 500 most important English words and phrases relating to Automotive Engineering, as well as a range of additional features which have been specially designed to help you to *really* understand and use the language of this specific area.

The main body of the book contains alphabetically organized dictionary-style entries for the key words and phrases of Automotive Engineering. These vocabulary items have been specially chosen to fully prepare you for the type of language that you will need in this field. Many are specialized terms that are very specific to this profession and area of study. Others are more common or general words and phrases that are often used in the context of Automotive Engineering.

Each word and phrase is explained clearly and precisely, in English that is easy to understand. In addition, each entry is illustrated with examples taken from the Collins Corpus. Of course, you will also find grammatical information about the way that the words and phrases behave.

In amongst the alphabetically organized entries, you will find valuable word-building features that will help you gain a better understanding of this area of English. For example, some features provide extra help with tricky pronunciations, while others pull together groups of related words that can usefully be learned as a set.

At the start of this book you will see lists of words and phrases, helpfully organized by topic area. You can use these lists to revise sets of vocabulary and to prepare for writing tasks. You can also download the audio for this book from www.collinselt.com/audio. This contains a recording of each headword in the book, followed by an example sentence. This will help you to learn and remember pronunciations of words and phrases. Furthermore, the exercise section at the end of this book gives you an opportunity to memorize important words and phrases, to assess what you have learned, and to work out which areas still need attention.

So whether you are studying Automotive Engineering, or you are already working in the field and intend to improve your career prospects, we are confident that *Collins COBUILD Key Words for Automotive Engineering* will equip you for success in the future.

Guide to Dictionary Entries

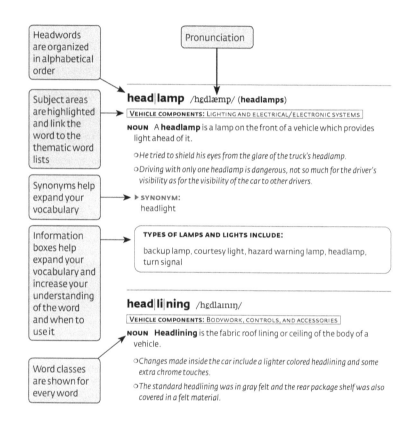

Headwords are organized in alphabetical order

Pronunciation

Subject areas are highlighted and link the word to the thematic word lists

Synonyms help expand your vocabulary

Information boxes help expand your vocabulary and increase your understanding of the word and when to use it

Word classes are shown for every word

head|lamp /hɛdlæmp/ (headlamps)

VEHICLE COMPONENTS: LIGHTING AND ELECTRICAL/ELECTRONIC SYSTEMS

NOUN A **headlamp** is a lamp on the front of a vehicle which provides light ahead of it.

○ He tried to shield his eyes from the glare of the truck's headlamp.

○ Driving with only one headlamp is dangerous, not so much for the driver's visibility as for the visibility of the car to other drivers.

▶ **SYNONYM:**
headlight

TYPES OF LAMPS AND LIGHTS INCLUDE:

backup lamp, courtesy light, hazard warning lamp, headlamp, turn signal

head|li|ning /hɛdlaɪnɪŋ/

VEHICLE COMPONENTS: BODYWORK, CONTROLS, AND ACCESSORIES

NOUN **Headlining** is the fabric roof lining or ceiling of the body of a vehicle.

○ Changes made inside the car include a lighter colored headlining and some extra chrome touches.

○ The standard headlining was in gray felt and the rear package shelf was also covered in a felt material.

Guide to Dictionary Entries

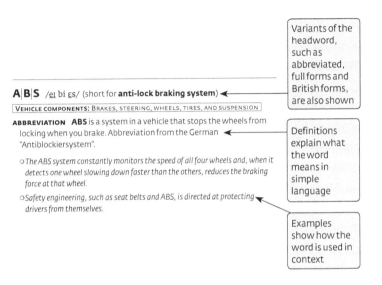

A|B|S /ˌeɪ bi ˈɛs/ (short for **anti-lock braking system**) ◄———

VEHICLE COMPONENTS: BRAKES, STEERING, WHEELS, TIRES, AND SUSPENSION

ABBREVIATION   **ABS** is a system in a vehicle that stops the wheels from
locking when you brake. Abbreviation from the German ◄———
"Antiblockiersystem".

 ○ *The ABS system constantly monitors the speed of all four wheels and, when it*
 detects one wheel slowing down faster than the others, reduces the braking
 force at that wheel.

 ○ *Safety engineering, such as seat belts and ABS, is directed at protecting* ◄———
 drivers from themselves.

Variants of the
headword,
such as
abbreviated,
full forms and
British forms,
are also shown

Definitions
explain what
the word
means in
simple
language

Examples
show how the
word is used in
context

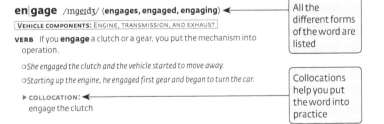

en|gage /ɪnˈɡeɪdʒ/ (**engages, engaged, engaging**) ◄———

VEHICLE COMPONENTS: ENGINE, TRANSMISSION, AND EXHAUST

VERB   If you **engage** a clutch or a gear, you put the mechanism into
operation.

 ○ *She engaged the clutch and the vehicle started to move away.*

 ○ *Starting up the engine, he engaged first gear and began to turn the car.*

 ▶ **COLLOCATION:** ◄———
 engage the clutch

All the
different forms
of the word are
listed

Collocations
help you put
the word into
practice

Guide to Pronunciation Symbols

Vowel Sounds

ɑ	calm, ah
ɑr	heart, far
æ	act, mass
ɑɪ	dive, cry
ɑɪər	fire, tire
ɑʊ	out, down
ɑʊər	flour, sour
ɛ	met, lend, pen
eɪ	say, weight
ɛər	fair, care
ɪ	fit, win
i	feed, me
ɪər	near, beard
ɒ	lot, spot
oʊ	note, coat
ɔ	claw, bought
ɔr	more, cord
ɔɪ	boy, joint
ʊ	could, stood
u	you, use
ʊər	lure, endure
ɜr	turn, third
ʌ	fund, must
ə	*the first vowel in a*bout
ər	*the first vowel in fo*rgotten
i	*the second vowel in ve*ry
u	*the second vowel in act*ual

Consonant Sounds

b	bed, rub
d	done, red
f	fit, if
g	good, dog
h	hat, horse
y	yellow, you
k	king, pick
l	lip, bill
ᵊl	handle, panel
m	mat, ram
n	not, tin
ᵊn	hidden, written
p	pay, lip
r	run, read
s	soon, bus
t	talk, bet
v	van, love
w	win, wool
ʍ	why, wheat
z	zoo, buzz
ʃ	ship, wish
ʒ	measure, leisure
ŋ	sing, working
tʃ	cheap, witch
θ	thin, myth
ð	then, other
dʒ	joy, bridge

Word lists

DESIGN AND PERFORMANCE
aerodynamic stability
bench test
BHP
bore-stroke ratio
bottom dead center
brake mean effective pressure
camber
capacity
compression
diagnostic testing
drag
eccentric
ergonomics
fuel consumption
handling
horsepower
hydroplaning
impact
indicator
indicator diagram
jackknife
model
NVH
oversteer
park
performance
reverse
ride
roadholding
roll center
rolling road
seat
skid
specific fuel consumption
spring rate
stall
steering geometry
stoichiometric ratio
suspension geometry
tick over
toe-in
toe-out
traction
tread
tune
turning circle
understeer
valve timing
volumetric efficiency
warm up
wheelbase

FUELS, OILS, EMISSIONS, AND OTHER FLUIDS
additive
alternative fuel
antifreeze
bio-diesel
bleed
carbon monoxide
cetane
cetane number
coolant
crude oil
detonation
dilution
emission
enrichment
exhaust analysis
exhaust emissions
explosion
fossil fuel
fuel
gasoline
grease
hydrocarbon
lead-free
lean mixture
LPG
mineral oil
multigrade oil
nitrogen oxides
octane number
pollutant
purge
rich mixture

MATERIALS
adhesion
adhesive
aluminum
chromium
elastomer
mild steel
nickel
rubber
stainless steel
steel
zinc

VEHICLE COMPONENTS
Bodywork, controls, and accessories

accelerator
adaptive cruise control
air bag
air-conditioning
airfoil
anti-vibration mounting
A-post
backrest
bench seat
bodywork
B-Post
brake pedal
bucket seat
bulkhead
bull bars
bumper
cab
central locking
chassis
choke
climate control
clutch pedal
coachwork
column shift
coupling
courtesy light
crew cab
cruise control
crush zone
dashboard
D-post
drawbar
electronic stability control system
engine management system
ergonomic
eye
fairing
fascia
firewall
float
folding top
fuel gauge
guttering
handbrake
hard top
header tank
headlining
headrest

head restraint
head-up display
hood
horn
instrument panel
jack
laminated glass
lamp
lap and diagonal belt
license plate
light
lock
monocoque
odometer
panel
parking sensor
passive restraint
pedal
power window
rearview mirror
roll cage
roof panel
safety cage
scuttle
seat
seat belt
seat belt tensioner
servo-mechanism
side impact bar
sill
skirt
spare wheel
spoiler
steering column
steering wheel
stick shift
sunroof
tailgate
traction control
trunk
turn signal
twist grip
underbody
vacuum servo
valve
ventilation
wheel arch
wheel well
windshield
windshield wiper
wiper blade

Brakes, steering, wheels, tires, and suspension
A-arm
ABS
adhesion
axle
backlash
belt
bias ply tire
blowout
brake
brake drum
brake fluid
brake lining
brake pad
brake servo
brake shoe
caliper
camber
carcass
caster
Caterpillar track
damper
diaphragm
disk brake
drum brake
electric retarder
elliptical spring
eye
hubcap
hydraulic brake
inboard brakes
independent suspension
inner tube
kingpin
live axle
lock
low-profile
MacPherson strut
manual steering
master cylinder
park
pneumatic tire
power steering
rack and pinion
radial ply tire
regenerative braking
retreaded tire
rim
snubber
suspension

tire
torsion bar
track rod
trailing arm
transmission brake
vacuum brake
wheel
wheel nut

Engine, transmission, and exhaust
air cleaner
air-cooled
air-fuel ratio
anti-knock
aspiration
automatic transmission
backfire
balk ring
beam axle
bearing cap
bell housing
belt
Bendix drive
bevel gear
big end
bleed
bleed screw
blow-back
blow-by
blower
boot
bore
cam
camshaft
capacity
carburetion
carburetor
cardan shaft
catalytic converter
chain and sprocket drive
change-speed gearbox
charge
CI engine
clearance volume
clutch
clutch disk
clutch slip
coil spring
combustion chamber
compression

compression ratio
compression stroke
connecting rod
constant mesh gearbox
constant velocity joint
cooling system
counter shaft
coupling
crank
crankcase
crankcase compression
crankpin
crankshaft
crankshaft end bearing
cut-out
cylinder
cylinder block
cylinder head
cylinder liner
dead center
diesel cycle
differential
direct injection
displacement
distributor
drain plug
drive shaft
drive train
dwell angle
eccentric
end float
engage
engine
engine bay
engine mount
exhaust gas recirculation
exhaust manifold
exhaust pipe
exhaust valve
fan
fan belt
feed pump
fender
filter
final drive
firing stroke
flexible joint
flywheel
four-stroke cycle
four-wheel drive
fuel injection

fuel pump
fuel rail
fuel system
fuel tank
gasket
gas tank
gearbox
gear ratio
gear train
glow plug
governor
half-shaft
horizontally opposed
hub
idle speed
ignition coil
ignition timing
indirect injection
induction
induction stroke
injection pump
injector
injector nozzle
intake manifold
intake valve
intercooler
internal combustion engine
jet
knock
layshaft
leaf spring
manifold
manual transmission
mean piston speed
motor
muffler
needle valve
neutral
normally aspirated
oil gauge
oil pan
oil pump
Otto cycle
overdrive
overhead valve
oversquare engine
particulate filter
piston
piston land
piston ring
piston skirt

plain bearing
planetary transmission
plug
poppet valve
prechamber
pre-ignition
PTO
quench
radiator
reciprocating engine
rocker arm
roller chain
rotor arm
scavenging
shock absorber
sleeve
spark ignition engine
spark plug
stabilizer bar
starter motor
stroke
supercharger
synchromesh gearbox
tappet
throttle
thrust bearing
timing
timing belt
timing chain
top dead center
torque converter
transfer box
transmission
turbocharger
twin camshaft
two-stroke cycle
universal joint
valve bounce
valve lift
valve seat
valve spring
valve train
V-belt
Venturi

**Lighting and electrical/
electronic systems**
alternator
antenna

backup light
battery
charge
circuit breaker
contact breaker
cut-out
dimmer switch
flat battery
fuel cell
fuel pump
fuse
hazard warning lamps
headlamp
ignition
immobilizer
in-car entertainment
jump lead
lead acid battery
relay
satellite navigation system
solenoid switch
terminal post
trip computer
wiring harness

VEHICLE TYPES
automatic
automobile
car
chassis dynamometer
coach
commercial vehicle
convertible
electric vehicle
hatchback
heavy goods vehicle
hybrid vehicle
motorcycle
motor scooter
off-highway vehicle
passenger car
semitrailer
soft top
track-laying vehicle
tractor
trailer
truck
van

A–Z

Aa

A-arm /eɪ ɑrm/ (**A-arms**)

VEHICLE COMPONENTS: BRAKES, STEERING, WHEELS, TIRES, AND SUSPENSION

NOUN An **A-arm** is part of a vehicle's suspension that consists of two rods in the shape of a letter A.

○ *The A-arm suspension consists of a pair of upper and lower lateral arms.*

○ *The standard suspension set-up at the front of the vehicle is MacPherson struts with lower A-arm and anti-roll bar.*

A|B|S /eɪ bi ɛs/ (short for **anti-lock braking system**)

VEHICLE COMPONENTS: BRAKES, STEERING, WHEELS, TIRES, AND SUSPENSION

ABBREVIATION **ABS** is a system in a vehicle that stops the wheels from locking when you brake. Abbreviation from the German "Antiblockiersystem."

○ *The ABS system constantly monitors the speed of all four wheels and, when it detects one wheel slowing down faster than the others, reduces the braking force at that wheel.*

○ *Safety engineering, such as seat belts and ABS, is directed at protecting drivers from themselves.*

PRONUNCIATION

Three-letter abbreviations are usually pronounced as separate letters with the stress on the last syllable.

ABS /eɪ bi ɛs/
BHP /bi eɪtʃ pi/
LPG /ɛl pi dʒi/
NVH /ɛn vi eɪtʃ/
PTO /pi ti oʊ/

ac|cel|er|a|tor /æksɛləreɪtər/ (**accelerators**)

VEHICLE COMPONENTS: BODYWORK, CONTROLS, AND ACCESSORIES

NOUN The **accelerator** in a vehicle is the pedal that controls the flow of gasoline to the engine, which you press with your foot in order to make the vehicle go faster.

○ *He eased his foot off the accelerator to slow down.*

○ *She put her foot down on the accelerator when the lights changed to green.*

a|dap|tive cruise con|trol (ABBR **ACC**) /ədæptɪv kruz kəntroʊl/

VEHICLE COMPONENTS: BODYWORK, CONTROLS, AND ACCESSORIES

NOUN **Adaptive cruise control** is an electronic control system in a vehicle that makes sure that the vehicle keeps a safe distance from vehicles in front.

○ *The car has adaptive cruise control, which maintains a set distance from the car in front to make highway driving less tiring.*

○ *Adaptive cruise control uses either radar or laser beams to keep a car a set distance behind the vehicle in front of it.*

ad|di|tive /ædɪtɪv/ (**additives**)

FUELS, OILS, EMISSIONS, AND OTHER FLUIDS

NOUN An **additive** is a small amount of chemical substance that is added to improve the quality of fuel.

○ *Oil refiners are required to use more ethanol as a gasoline additive for cleaner-burning fuel.*

○ *Oil companies are being sued because of the additive MTBE, which has been found to pollute water.*

ad|he|sion[1] /ædhiʒ³n/

VEHICLE COMPONENTS: BRAKES, STEERING, WHEELS, TIRES, AND SUSPENSION

NOUN **Adhesion** is the ability of a vehicle's tire to stick firmly to the road.

○ *Better driving equipment will improve track adhesion in slippery conditions.*

○ *The cars are equipped with a device which increases rear tire adhesion.*

> **WORD FAMILY**
>
> **adhesion** NOUN ○ *Good tires will increase adhesion to the road surface.*
>
> **adhesive** NOUN ○ *The two surfaces are joined with an adhesive.*
>
> Both of these words come from the verb **adhere**, which means "to stick."

---

ad|he|sion² /ædhiːʒən/

`MATERIALS`

NOUN **Adhesion** is the ability of two surfaces to stick firmly together using an adhesive.

○ *This material has amazing adhesion to almost any surface, wet or dry.*

○ *It is difficult to achieve good paint adhesion to this material.*

---

ad|he|sive /ædhiːsɪv/ (**adhesives**)

`MATERIALS`

NOUN An **adhesive** is a substance that is used to make two surfaces stick firmly together.

○ *When using adhesives, ensure that all surfaces to be joined are clean and dry.*

○ *Solvents are present in paints, degreasing solutions, and adhesives.*

---

aer|o|dy|nam|ic sta|bil|i|ty /ɛəroʊdaɪnæmɪk stəbɪlɪti/

`DESIGN AND PERFORMANCE`

NOUN **Aerodynamic stability** is the way that a moving vehicle reacts to changes in air caused by passing vehicles.

○ *The suspension automatically lowers the car at high speeds for better fuel economy and aerodynamic stability.*

○ *This device, positioned under the car, helps reduce lift and increases aerodynamic stability.*

A

air bag /ɛər bæg/ (air bags)

VEHICLE COMPONENTS: BODYWORK, CONTROLS, AND ACCESSORIES

NOUN An **air bag** is a safety device in a car that automatically fills with air if the car crashes, and is designed to protect the people in the car when they are thrown forward in the crash.

○ Research shows that seat belts prevent more deaths than air bags in road accidents.

○ Children under age 12 should not ride in the front seat of vehicles equipped with air bags.

▶ **COLLOCATIONS:**
driver's air bag
driver's side air bag
passenger side air bag

air clean|er /ɛər klinər/ (air cleaners)

VEHICLE COMPONENTS: ENGINE, TRANSMISSION, AND EXHAUST

NOUN An **air cleaner** or **air filter** is any device that stops particles that are present in the air from entering air-breathing machinery.

○ Special features include an air cleaner that filters exhaust emissions from other cars.

○ The carburetor breathes through an oil bath air cleaner.

air-con|di|tion|ing (ABBR AC) /ɛər kəndɪʃənɪŋ/

VEHICLE COMPONENTS: BODYWORK, CONTROLS, AND ACCESSORIES

NOUN **Air-conditioning** is a method of providing vehicles with cool dry air.

○ Because of the hot climate, all cars are equipped with air-conditioning.

○ It was hot in the car, even with the air-conditioning turned to its coldest setting.

▶ **COLLOCATION:**
air-conditioning system

air-cooled /ɛər kuld/

VEHICLE COMPONENTS: ENGINE, TRANSMISSION, AND EXHAUST

ADJECTIVE An **air-cooled** engine is prevented from getting too hot when it is running by cool air that passes over it, rather than being cooled by a liquid.

○ *The car was powered by a four-cylinder air-cooled engine.*

○ *The car's air-cooled engine has been replaced by a water-cooled version.*

▶ COLLOCATION:
air-cooled engine

air|foil (BRIT **aerofoil**) /ɛərfɔɪl/ (**airfoils**)

VEHICLE COMPONENTS: BODYWORK, CONTROLS, AND ACCESSORIES

NOUN An **airfoil** is a flat shape such as a wing that is intended to produce a particular effect from the flow of air.

○ *Engineers have made a modification to the racing car's airfoil wings to increase the downward force.*

○ *The off-road vehicle had a giant rear airfoil that actually doubled as a roof rack.*

air-fuel ra|ti|o /ɛər fyuəl reɪʃou/ (**air-fuel ratios**)

VEHICLE COMPONENTS: ENGINE, TRANSMISSION, AND EXHAUST

NOUN The **air-fuel ratio** or **air-fuel delivery ratio** is the ratio of air to fuel that is taken in by an engine.

○ *The engine allows for a particularly low air-fuel ratio during warm-up to reduce emissions of unburned fuel.*

○ *The electronic control unit recalculates the air-fuel ratio for the most efficient operation.*

al|ter|na|tive fuel /ɔltɜrnətɪv fyuəl/ (**alternative fuels**)

FUELS, OILS, EMISSIONS, AND OTHER FLUIDS

NOUN An **alternative fuel** is any automotive fuel other than gasoline and diesel fuel.

○ *The number of trucks, cars, and buses running on alternative fuels will help reduce pollution in the region.*

○ *A 40 percent tax deduction is offered on company cars powered by alternative fuels.*

---

al|ter|na|tor /ɔltərneɪtər/ (**alternators**)

VEHICLE COMPONENTS: LIGHTING AND ELECTRICAL/ELECTRONIC SYSTEMS

NOUN An **alternator** is a device used in a car that creates an electrical current that changes direction as it flows.

○ *It is the responsibility of the alternator to ensure that the battery is fully charged and ready to go.*

○ *Most alternator difficulties are caused by bad connections or not having the drive belt tension correctly adjusted.*

---

a|lu|mi|num (BRIT **aluminium**) /əlumɪnəm/

MATERIALS

NOUN **Aluminum** is a chemical element that is used in alloy form to make a lightweight metal, used, for example, for vehicle bodywork.

○ *The cars will have lightweight aluminum bodies to improve the power to weight ratio, giving better acceleration.*

○ *The traditional aluminum windshield surround has been replaced by a chunky, black steel frame.*

> **US/UK ENGLISH**
>
> The form **aluminum** is used in American English. The stress is on the second syllable.
>
> The form **aluminium** is used in British English. The stress is on the third syllable.

---

an|ten|na (In BRIT use **aerial**) /æntɛnə/ (**antennae**)

VEHICLE COMPONENTS: LIGHTING AND ELECTRICAL/ELECTRONIC SYSTEMS

NOUN An **antenna** is a device or a piece of wire that sends and receives radio signals.

○ *The car's CD player has an AM/FM radio with a telescoping antenna and station presets.*

○ *The three antennae mounted on his car boost the reception of his wireless network.*

PRONUNCIATION

Note the irregular plural of this word and the way it is pronounced:
antennae /æntɛni/

---

an|ti|freeze /æntifriz/

FUELS, OILS, EMISSIONS, AND OTHER FLUIDS

NOUN **Antifreeze** is a liquid that is added to the cooling water of an engine to stop it from freezing in cold weather.

○ *The cooling system can be filled with an antifreeze mixture for winter protection.*

○ *These chemicals are used in car antifreeze to stop corrosion.*

WORD BUILDER
anti- = against

The prefix **anti-** often appears in words connected with preventing things: **antifreeze**, **antiknock**, **antivibration**.

---

an|ti-knock /æntɪ nɒk/

VEHICLE COMPONENTS: ENGINE, TRANSMISSION, AND EXHAUST

ADJECTIVE An **anti-knock** agent helps to stop an engine from knocking, making it function more smoothly.

○ *Car manufacturers are designing cars which can use anti-knock agents other than lead, because of the danger to health.*

○ *Petroleum refiners have added more light hydrocarbon components to their gasoline mixtures to make up for the loss of lead as an anti-knock additive.*

A

an|ti-vi|bra|tion mount|ing /ˌænti vaɪbreɪʃⁿn maʊntɪŋ/
(**anti-vibration mountings**)

VEHICLE COMPONENTS: BODYWORK, CONTROLS, AND ACCESSORIES

NOUN An **anti-vibration mounting** is a flexible support for an engine that reduces the amount of noise and vibration that passes to the vehicle chassis.

○ *A highly important function of an anti-vibration mounting is to reduce noise.*

○ *Isolating engine vibrations from the main body of the car is usually achieved by the use of rubber anti-vibration mountings.*

A-post /eɪ poʊst/ (**A-posts**)

VEHICLE COMPONENTS: BODYWORK, CONTROLS, AND ACCESSORIES

NOUN An **A-post** is part of the bodywork of a vehicle that supports the roof at the front corner of the passenger compartment next to the windshield.

○ *The A-post at the front of the door frame was damaged.*

○ *A large section of each front fender, above the wheel arch and right back to the A-post had to be removed.*

> **RELATED WORDS**
>
> Compare an **A-post** with a **B-post**, against which the front door closes, and a **D-post**, against which the rear door closes.

as|pi|ra|tion /ˌæspɪreɪʃⁿn/

VEHICLE COMPONENTS: ENGINE, TRANSMISSION, AND EXHAUST

NOUN **Aspiration** is the breathing or induction process of an engine.

○ *Modifications to the intake and exhaust systems help the engine's aspiration.*

○ *Induction, compression, ignition, and exhaust. These are what we call the cycles of aspiration of a four-stroke engine.*

au|to|mat|ic /ˌɔtəmætɪk/ (**automatics**)

VEHICLE TYPES

NOUN An **automatic** is a vehicle with automatic transmission.

○ *If you passed your test in an automatic, you must return to do it all over again in a manual car.*

○ *Since his accident, he drives an automatic, which he steers with one arm.*

---

au|to|mat|ic trans|mis|sion[1] /ɔtəmætɪk trænzmɪʃⁿn/

| VEHICLE COMPONENTS: ENGINE, TRANSMISSION, AND EXHAUST |

NOUN A vehicle that is equipped with **automatic transmission** has a gear system in which the gears change automatically.

○ *The car is available with a 1.8 liter gasoline engine and manual or automatic transmission.*

○ *The vehicles are very easy to drive, with automatic transmission and power steering.*

---

au|to|mat|ic trans|mis|sion[2] /ɔtəmætɪk trænzmɪʃⁿn/

| VEHICLE COMPONENTS: ENGINE, TRANSMISSION, AND EXHAUST |

NOUN **Automatic transmission** is a system for moving a vehicle that uses a friction drive that varies its speed, such as a belt with expanding pulley.

○ *The car is is a liquid-cooled four-stroke with fully automatic transmission.*

○ *If you have to do much driving in town you will find an automatic transmission makes you much less tired.*

---

au|to|mo|bile /ɔtəməbil/ (**automobiles**)

| VEHICLE TYPES |

NOUN An **automobile** is a private passenger car.

○ *The company specializes in affordable automobiles with low emissions.*

○ *The ruling requires the fuel companies to supply enough ultra-clean fuels to meet the needs of the new cleaner automobiles.*

▶ COLLOCATIONS:
automobile industry
automobile maker
automobile manufacturer

ax|le /æksəl/ (**axles**)

VEHICLE COMPONENTS: BRAKES, STEERING, WHEELS, TIRES, AND SUSPENSION

NOUN An **axle** is a rod connecting a pair of wheels on a vehicle.

○ *Front-wheel drive axles have CV joints at each end.*

○ *A car with equal weight on its front and rear axles is better balanced and thus more agile.*

▶ **COLLOCATIONS:**
front axle
rear axle

Bb

back|fire /ˈbækfaɪər/ (backfires, backfired, backfiring)

VERB When a vehicle or its engine **backfires**, it produces an explosion in the exhaust pipe.

- ○ *The vehicle tends to backfire when slowing down, making a sound like a gunshot.*
- ○ *The research aims to reduce the tendency for the engine to backfire, which is a challenge in conventional engines.*

back|lash /ˈbæklæʃ/

NOUN **Backlash** is loss of motion between the input and output of a mechanical system, such as that caused by looseness or bending.

- ○ *Because the rolling elements are under constant preload, the roller drive is not subject to backlash when torque is suddenly removed or reversed.*
- ○ *The amount of backlash in the steering made it difficult to control the vehicle on the bends in the narrow streets.*

back|rest /ˈbækrɛst/ (backrests)

NOUN The **backrest** of a seat in a vehicle is the part that you rest your back on.

- ○ *The front seat is on slides, with a reclining backrest.*
- ○ *For carrying extra long loads, the divided rear-seat backrest folds flat in a moment.*

B

back|up light /bækʌp laɪt/ (backup lights)

VEHICLE COMPONENTS: LIGHTING AND ELECTRICAL/ELECTRONIC SYSTEMS

NOUN A **backup light** is a lamp used to provide light behind a vehicle, particularly when reversing.

○ *The color of the light from a backup light shall be white, in accordance with regulations.*

○ *Backup lights must not be continuously lit when the vehicle is in forward motion.*

▶ SYNONYM:
backup lamp

balk ring (BRIT **baulk ring**) /bɔːk rɪŋ/ (balk rings)

VEHICLE COMPONENTS: ENGINE, TRANSMISSION, AND EXHAUST

NOUN A **balk ring** is a rotating part of a gearbox that prevents the gears from engaging too early.

○ *The balk ring in a gearbox wears out very quickly so engagement can become a problem on that gear.*

○ *The 3rd gear shifts had become a bit crunchy, indicating wear on the 3rd gear balk ring.*

▶ SYNONYM:
blocking ring

bat|ter|y /bætəri/ (batteries)

VEHICLE COMPONENTS: LIGHTING AND ELECTRICAL/ELECTRONIC SYSTEMS

NOUN A car **battery** is a rectangular box containing acid that is found in a car engine. It provides the electricity that is needed to start the car.

○ *If you leave the lights on, you will run down the battery.*

○ *The solar cell will trickle-charge your car battery while the car is left standing for long periods.*

TALKING ABOUT THE BATTERY

If you put electricity into a battery, you **charge** it or **recharge** it.

If something uses all the electricity from a battery, it **drains** it.

If you **disconnect** the battery, you stop it being connected to the electrical system.

---

beam ax|le /biːm æksᵊl/ (**beam axles**)

VEHICLE COMPONENTS: ENGINE, TRANSMISSION, AND EXHAUST

NOUN A **beam axle** is a rigid beam which connects a nearside (= on the side near the pavement) wheel and an offside (= on the side away from the pavement) wheel.

○ *This kind of hub is used mainly on larger vehicles, where a beam axle is fitted instead of independent suspension.*

○ *This model features a multi-link beam axle at the back to help counter rear-end instability.*

bear|ing cap¹ /bɛərɪŋ kæp/ (**bearing caps**)

VEHICLE COMPONENTS: ENGINE, TRANSMISSION, AND EXHAUST

NOUN A **bearing cap** is a rigid, semi-circular part that fits around one half of a bearing and secures it.

○ *Oil the new lower bearing and install it in the bearing cap.*

○ *Make sure you don't over-tighten the bearing cap. Otherwise you might cause the bearing to seize.*

bear|ing cap² /bɛərɪŋ kæp/ (**bearing caps**)

VEHICLE COMPONENTS: ENGINE, TRANSMISSION, AND EXHAUST

NOUN A **bearing cap** is a removable disk that prevents unwanted particles from entering into the place where the bearings are contained.

○ *To replace main bearings, remove the bearing cap and take out the worn lower shell.*

○ *You should remove the main bearing cap and pull the oil seal out.*

bell hous|ing /bɛl haʊzɪŋ/ (**bell housings**)

VEHICLE COMPONENTS: ENGINE, TRANSMISSION, AND EXHAUST

NOUN A **bell housing** is a bell-shaped extension of an engine crankcase, that contains the flywheel and the clutch.

○ *A clutch explosion can destroy the bell housing and body sheet metal, and injure the driver.*

○ *He regained speed only to slow down again when the bell housing cracked.*

belt¹ /bɛlt/ (belts)

VEHICLE COMPONENTS: ENGINE, TRANSMISSION, AND EXHAUST

NOUN A **belt** is a circular strip of rubber that is used to drive moving parts in a vehicle.

○ On some engines, the water pump may not be driven by the same belt as the alternator.

○ The turning disk is connected by a drive belt to an electric motor.

belt² /bɛlt/ (belts)

VEHICLE COMPONENTS: BRAKES, STEERING, WHEELS, TIRES, AND SUSPENSION

NOUN A **belt** is continuous reinforcing around the outside of a tire, usually made from steel or a man-made fiber.

○ They are developing a new fiber for tire belt reinforcement.

○ The belt on these tires is lighter in weight than a conventional woven steel cord belt.

bench seat /bɛntʃ sit/ (bench seats)

VEHICLE COMPONENTS: BODYWORK, CONTROLS, AND ACCESSORIES

NOUN A **bench seat** is a wide vehicle seat for more than one person.

○ The car seats five, with individually molded seats for the rear three passengers instead of the normal bench seat.

○ There is plenty of legroom for the driver and front passenger, and a relatively spacious rear bench seat is provided.

bench test /bɛntʃ tɛst/ (bench tests)

DESIGN AND PERFORMANCE

NOUN A **bench test** is an operating test carried out on an engine or other major part removed from a vehicle.

○ Mechanics did a bench test on the fuel-control unit and found that it was mis-rigged.

○ Your dealer should remove the starter motor and do a bench test on it.

Ben|dix drive /bɛndɪks draɪv/ (**Bendix drives**)

VEHICLE COMPONENTS: ENGINE, TRANSMISSION, AND EXHAUST

NOUN A **Bendix drive** is a drive consisting of a pinion wheel (= a gear with a small number of teeth) carried on a shaft. The shaft rotates, causing the pinion to move.

○ *The standard Bendix drive depends on inertia to provide meshing of the drive.*

○ *To start the engine, the Bendix drive starts automatically when the starter motor begins to turn.*

bev|el gear /bɛvəl gɪər/ (**bevel gears**)

VEHICLE COMPONENTS: ENGINE, TRANSMISSION, AND EXHAUST

NOUN A **bevel gear** is a gear wheel with teeth cut in such a way that two wheels working together have shafts at an angle to each other, usually a right angle.

○ *One of the bevel gear boxes in the propeller drive failed.*

○ *Both valves and camshaft are overhead, and the latter is driven by a spiral bevel gear.*

B|H|P /bi eɪtʃ pi/ (short for **brake horsepower**)

DESIGN AND PERFORMANCE

ABBREVIATION **BHP** is a measure of engine power that is approximately equivalent to three quarters of a kilowatt.

○ *Increasing the speed at 125 BHP from 3600–3800 rpm increased the oil sump temperature only about 4 degrees.*

○ *Output from the engine is rated at 200 BHP at 6000 rpm.*

bi|as ply tire (In BRIT use **crossply tyre**) /baɪəs plaɪ taɪər/ (**bias ply tires**)

VEHICLE COMPONENTS: BRAKES, STEERING, WHEELS, TIRES, AND SUSPENSION

NOUN A **bias ply tire** is a tire constructed on a base of diagonally laid layers of fabric.

○ *A small bias ply tire can carry more weight than a radial tire of similar size.*

○ *The bias ply tires have plies running at 45 degrees to the center line of the tread, alternating in direction with each layer.*

B

big end /bɪɡ ɛnd/ (**big ends**)

VEHICLE COMPONENTS: ENGINE, TRANSMISSION, AND EXHAUST

NOUN A **big end** is the end of a connecting rod that engages with a crankshaft.

- ○ The top end of the connecting rod is called the small end, and the bottom end is called the big end.
- ○ He crawled under the engine every 15 miles or so to examine the big end for overheating.

bi|o-die|sel /baɪoʊ dizᵊl/

FUELS, OILS, EMISSIONS, AND OTHER FLUIDS

NOUN **Bio-diesel** is diesel fuel made from biological or natural sources.

- ○ Some car manufacturers have complained that 100 percent bio-diesel (made from vegetable oil or animal fats) upsets engine management systems.
- ○ New environmental legislation means that, by the end of the year, just under 5 percent of all diesel must be bio-diesel.

bleed¹ /blid/ (**bleeds**)

VEHICLE COMPONENTS: ENGINE, TRANSMISSION, AND EXHAUST

NOUN A **bleed** is a valve or other way of emptying a system of fluid, or reducing pressure.

- ○ The fuel system can be emptied using a bleed.
- ○ All carburetors have air bleeds and vents to control air flow through the carburetor passages.

bleed² /blid/ (**bleeds, bled, bleeding**)

FUELS, OILS, EMISSIONS, AND OTHER FLUIDS

VERB If you **bleed** a fuel system, you empty it of fluid in order to work on it or refill it with fresh fluid.

- ○ You'll need to bleed the fuel system to make sure that no remnant of the contaminated diesel is still in the system.
- ○ The only thing I knew how to do on the engine was to bleed the fuel system.

▶ COLLOCATION:
bleed the system

bleed screw /blid skru/ (**bleed screws**)

NOUN A **bleed screw** is a type of tap or valve that helps to drain a hydraulic system, such as a brake system.

○ The pressure vessel was fitted with a bleed screw and thermometer pocket.

○ A vacuum bleeder pulls fluid from the master cylinder through the bleed screw by suction.

blow-back /blou bæk/

NOUN **Blow-back** is when the air flow through a carburetor suddenly changes direction. This is often caused by incorrect ignition.

○ The tank design allows full fuel flow from the gas pump directly into the tank without blow-back.

○ As the throttle is opened, there is heavy blow-back of fuel from the carburetor air intake.

blow-by /blou baɪ/

NOUN **Blow-by** is unwanted leakage of gas under pressure, such as that from a piston or its sealing rings.

○ The blow-by that occurs when too much pressure from the combustion chamber leaks into the crankcase needs to escape somewhere.

○ All piston engines experience blow-by of compressed gas past the piston rings.

blow|er /blouər/ (**blowers**)

NOUN A **blower** is an exhaust turbocharger.

○ The exhaust handling system includes a dilution air filter and a blower to induce flow.

○ We call them "blowers" because they blow pressurized air into the engine. Technical people prefer to call them "turbochargers", though.

blow|out /ˈbloʊaʊt/ (**blowouts**)

VEHICLE COMPONENTS: BRAKES, STEERING, WHEELS, TIRES, AND SUSPENSION

NOUN If you have a **blowout** while you are driving a car, one of the tires suddenly bursts.

○ *A truck traveling south had a blowout and crashed.*

○ *Wider rims are used to reduce tire damage during a flat or blowout.*

bod|y|work /ˈbɒdiwɜrk/

VEHICLE COMPONENTS: BODYWORK, CONTROLS, AND ACCESSORIES

NOUN The **bodywork** of a vehicle is the outside part of it.

○ *Even hitting a traffic cone at high speed can make a large dent in a car's bodywork.*

○ *The car has a 1.1-liter engine and comes with five-door as well as three-door bodywork.*

boot /ˈbut/ (**boots**)

VEHICLE COMPONENTS: ENGINE, TRANSMISSION, AND EXHAUST

NOUN A **boot** is a thin, flexible tube, often shaped like a concertina, that stops dirt and liquids from entering the mechanical parts of a vehicle, such as shaft couplings.

○ *Each of the joints is covered by a boot.*

○ *Fold back the dust boot which covers the steering shaft joint.*

▶ SYNONYMS:
   bellows
   gaiter

bore¹ /ˈbɔr/ (**bores**)

VEHICLE COMPONENTS: ENGINE, TRANSMISSION, AND EXHAUST

NOUN The **bore** is the internal diameter of the cylinder of an engine or pump.

○ *The engine is a three-liter unit with an 83 x 90mm bore and stroke.*

○ *The four-cylinder, four-stroke engine has a bore of 80mm.*

bore² /bɔr/ (bores)

VEHICLE COMPONENTS: ENGINE, TRANSMISSION, AND EXHAUST

NOUN The **bore** is the cylinder wall of an engine.

○ *The engine has new cylinder heads and pistons fitted to a smaller aluminum block with larger cylinder bores.*

○ *Lubricate the cylinder bores with a light spray of oil into each plug hole.*

▶ COLLOCATION:
cylinder bore

bore³ /bɔr/ (bores, bored, boring)

VEHICLE COMPONENTS: ENGINE, TRANSMISSION, AND EXHAUST

VERB If you **bore** a hole in something, you make a deep round hole in it using a special tool.

○ *You'll have to bore a hole in the engine mounting.*

○ *"We bore a big hole, but drill a smaller one," the machinist explained.*

▶ COLLOCATION:
bore a hole

bore⁴ /bɔr/ (bores, bored, boring)

VEHICLE COMPONENTS: ENGINE, TRANSMISSION, AND EXHAUST

VERB If you **bore** a cylinder in an engine, you increase the size of the cylinder bore to accept the piston, and so increase displacement.

○ *Next, bore the cylinder to fit the piston in.*

○ *Remove the cylinder and bore it to the precise dimensions to obtain proper piston clearance.*

▶ COLLOCATION:
bore the cylinder

bore-stroke ra|ti|o /bɔr stroʊk reɪʃoʊ/ (bore-stroke ratios)

DESIGN AND PERFORMANCE

NOUN The **bore-stroke ratio** is the ratio of bore to stroke. A ratio of 1:1 is referred to informally as square.

B

○ Your engine's bore-stroke ratio plays a vital part in the way it produces power.

○ The bore-stroke ratio and the cylinder volume affect the exhaust emissions and the fuel consumption of an engine.

---

bot|tom dead cen|ter (ABBR **BDC**) /bɒtəm dɛd sɛntər/

DESIGN AND PERFORMANCE

NOUN **Bottom dead center** is the point at which the piston of an engine is nearest to the axis of the crankshaft. On a vertical engine, this is the lowest point that the piston reaches.

○ When the piston reaches bottom dead center, it starts to move upwards.

○ During the compression stroke, the piston moves up from bottom dead center.

B-Post /biː poʊst/ (**B-Posts**)

VEHICLE COMPONENTS: BODYWORK, CONTROLS, AND ACCESSORIES

NOUN A **B-post** is part of the bodywork of a vehicle that supports the roof and against which the front door closes.

○ The B-posts are located between the front and rear doors of a vehicle.

○ The B-post between the front and back doors is replaced by a central post in the middle.

---

brake¹ /breɪk/ (**brakes**)

VEHICLE COMPONENTS: BRAKES, STEERING, WHEELS, TIRES, AND SUSPENSION

NOUN **Brakes** are devices in a vehicle that make it go slower or stop.

○ Parts of the brake that may need replacement include linings and calipers.

○ The car tends to skid from the rear if the brakes are applied hard.

> **USING THE BRAKES IN A VEHICLE**
>
> If you want to slow down or stop a vehicle, you **put on** the brakes or (formal) **apply** the brakes.
>
> If you want to slow down a little, you can **tap** the brakes, **squeeze** the brakes, or **touch** the brakes.

If someone is traveling fast and suddenly puts on the brakes, you can say that they **slam on** the brakes or **hit** the brakes.

If someone presses and releases the brakes repeatedly, you can say that they **pump** the brakes.

---

brake² /breɪk/ (**brakes, braked, braking**)

VEHICLE COMPONENTS: BRAKES, STEERING, WHEELS, TIRES, AND SUSPENSION

TRANSITIVE/INTRANSITIVE VERB When a vehicle or its driver **brakes**, or when a driver **brakes** a vehicle, the driver makes it slow down or stop by using the brakes.

○ He heard tires squeal as the car braked to avoid a collision.

○ She was forced to brake sharply as the other car cut in front of her.

---

brake drum /breɪk drʌm/ (**brake drums**)

VEHICLE COMPONENTS: BRAKES, STEERING, WHEELS, TIRES, AND SUSPENSION

NOUN A **brake drum** is a closed cylinder attached to a vehicle wheel, against which a brake shoe presses to make the vehicle go slower or stop.

○ The inside surface of the brake drum must be smooth and uniform so that the brake shoe can be applied against it.

○ The brake shoes are forced by hydraulic wheel cylinders against the inner surface of the rotating brake drum.

---

brake flu|id /breɪk fluɪd/ (**brake fluids**)

VEHICLE COMPONENTS: BRAKES, STEERING, WHEELS, TIRES, AND SUSPENSION

NOUN **Brake fluid** is the fluid contained in a hydraulic brake system.

○ The rear offside brake was leaking brake fluid.

○ The braking system in a car uses a brake fluid to transmit the pressure from the pedal cylinder to the wheel cylinder.

B

brake lin|ing /breɪk laɪnɪŋ/ (**brake linings**)

VEHICLE COMPONENTS: BRAKES, STEERING, WHEELS, TIRES, AND SUSPENSION

NOUN A **brake lining** is friction material attached to the face of a brake shoe, to cause frictional force when the brake shoe makes contact with the brake drum.

○ A brake lining can be bonded or riveted to a metal brake shoe.

○ The aim of the inspection is to check and replace brake linings before they wear badly, allowing brake shoe metal to be exposed.

brake mean ef|fec|tive pres|sure (ABBR **BMEP**) /breɪk min ɪfɛktɪv prɛʃər/

DESIGN AND PERFORMANCE

NOUN **Brake mean effective pressure** is a calculation of the engine cylinder pressure that would give the measured brake horsepower.

○ Brake mean effective pressure is an indication of engine efficiency regardless of capacity or engine speed.

○ Brake mean effective pressure is a widely used measure of the load imposed on an engine.

brake pad /breɪk pæd/ (**brake pads**)

VEHICLE COMPONENTS: BRAKES, STEERING, WHEELS, TIRES, AND SUSPENSION

NOUN A **brake pad** is a thin block that presses onto the disk in a disk brake in order to make a vehicle go slower or stop.

○ New more durable brake pad material increases the life of brake linings by 50 percent.

○ When the brake pedal is applied, the brake pads are forced by hydraulic pressure against the brake disk.

brake pe|dal /breɪk pɛdəl/ (**brake pedals**)

VEHICLE COMPONENTS: BODYWORK, CONTROLS, AND ACCESSORIES

NOUN The **brake pedal** is the pedal that you press with your foot in order to make a vehicle go slower or stop.

○ When the driver puts his foot on the brake pedal, the system automatically applies the optimum pressure required to avoid hitting the car in front.

○ *The rear brake lights produce varying degrees of red light depending on the level of force applied to the brake pedal.*

b

---

brake ser|vo /breɪk sɜrvoʊ/ (**brake servos**)

VEHICLE COMPONENTS: BRAKES, STEERING, WHEELS, TIRES, AND SUSPENSION

NOUN The **brake servo** is a device for increasing the pressure of the driver's foot on the brake pedal.

○ *The addition of a brake servo does not improve braking performance, it simply helps with the amount of force that is needed to operate the brakes.*

○ *Just as important to the car's performance are the four piston front brake calipers and a brake servo system offering improved pedal feel.*

---

brake shoe /breɪk ʃu/ (**brake shoes**)

VEHICLE COMPONENTS: BRAKES, STEERING, WHEELS, TIRES, AND SUSPENSION

NOUN The **brake shoe** is the part of a drum brake to which the friction lining is attached.

○ *The brake lining gradually wears away as the brake shoe assembly is used to brake a vehicle.*

○ *The brake pad is connected to a pad mounting surface of the brake shoe.*

---

buck|et seat /bʌkɪt sit/ (**bucket seats**)

VEHICLE COMPONENTS: BODYWORK, CONTROLS, AND ACCESSORIES

NOUN A **bucket seat** is a seat for one person in a vehicle which has rounded sides that partly enclose and support the body.

○ *He climbed into the car and settled into the passenger side bucket seat.*

○ *A headrest from a bench seat won't fit a bucket seat.*

---

bulk|head /bʌlkhɛd/ (**bulkheads**)

VEHICLE COMPONENTS: BODYWORK, CONTROLS, AND ACCESSORIES

NOUN A **bulkhead** is a panel that separates the engine compartment from the passenger compartment of a vehicle.

○ *The steering rack in this car is welded to the bulkhead of the engine compartment.*

B

○ The engine, transmission, and front suspension are mounted to a steel
subframe bolted to the bulkhead.

---

bull bars /bʊl bɑrz/

VEHICLE COMPONENTS: BODYWORK, CONTROLS, AND ACCESSORIES

NOUN **Bull bars** are the strong bars that protect the lamps and other
front parts of a vehicle.

○ The EU directive aims to make cars more pedestrian-friendly, and will include
a ban on bull bars on cars.

○ The front bull bars of the SUV had become embedded in the tree in the crash.

---

bump|er /bʌmpər/ (bumpers)

VEHICLE COMPONENTS: BODYWORK, CONTROLS, AND ACCESSORIES

NOUN **Bumpers** are bars at the front and back of a vehicle that protect it
if it bumps into something.

○ He tied a tow rope to the car's bumper and prepared to move it with his truck.

○ The spare tire was mounted to the rear bumper to create more trunk room.

▶ **COLLOCATIONS:**
front bumper
rear bumper

Cc

---

cab /kæb/ (cabs)

VEHICLE COMPONENTS: BODYWORK, CONTROLS, AND ACCESSORIES

NOUN The **cab** of a truck is the front part in which the driver sits.

○ *She climbed into the cab, and the truck started off again.*

○ *The truck has additional load space over the driver's cab.*

---

cal|i|per (BRIT **calliper**) /kælɪpər/ (calipers)

VEHICLE COMPONENTS: BRAKES, STEERING, WHEELS, TIRES, AND SUSPENSION

NOUN A **caliper** is the mechanism in a disk brake system that uses a pinching action to cause the brake pads to press onto the disk.

○ *The rear brakes have a 220mm floating disk with a single caliper.*

○ *The job of the caliper is to squeeze the brake pads against the rotor surface in order to slow the car.*

---

cam /kæm/ (cams)

VEHICLE COMPONENTS: ENGINE, TRANSMISSION, AND EXHAUST

NOUN A **cam** is a shaped part in machinery such as an engine that rotates in order to cause another part to move or lift.

○ *A circular cam is fitted off-center on the driving shaft and produces an oscillating movement in the follower.*

○ *Cams are used to change rotary motion into either reciprocating motion or oscillating motion.*

cam|ber¹ /ˈkæmbər/ (cambers)

VEHICLE COMPONENTS: BRAKES, STEERING, WHEELS, TIRES, AND SUSPENSION

NOUN **Camber** is the angle of the plane of a wheel in relation to the vertical plane of symmetry of a vehicle. Camber is considered positive if the wheels lean out towards the top, and negative if they slope inward.

○ To enhance rear-end grip, he gave the rear wheels three degrees' negative camber, leaning inwards at the top.

○ This system automatically adjusts the camber in the rear wheels to allow the maximum amount of tire-surface-to-road-surface contact while the race car is cornering.

▶ COLLOCATIONS:
negative camber
positive camber

cam|ber² /ˈkæmbər/ (cambers)

DESIGN AND PERFORMANCE

NOUN A **camber** is a gradual downward slope from the center of a road to each side of it.

○ You have to be really careful driving on hills, where the camber changes all the time.

○ On the icy road, the slightest camber caused the four-wheel drive to drift off line.

cam|shaft /ˈkæmʃæft/ (camshafts)

VEHICLE COMPONENTS: ENGINE, TRANSMISSION, AND EXHAUST

NOUN A **camshaft** is a rod in an engine that works to change circular motion into motion up and down or from side to side.

○ A camshaft determines how and when the engine valves open.

○ Conventional fuel injection in a diesel engine involves a pump driven via a camshaft from the engine.

ca|pac|i|ty¹ /kəpǽsɪti/

VEHICLE COMPONENTS: ENGINE, TRANSMISSION, AND EXHAUST

NOUN The **capacity** of an engine is its size or power, expressed in Europe as cubic centimeters or liters, and in the US as cubic inches.

○ *The amount of road tax you pay should depend on the size and engine capacity of your car.*

○ *This model has a fuel-injected in-line three-cylinder engine with a cubic capacity of 140 cubic inches.*

▶ COLLOCATIONS:
  cubic capacity
  engine capacity

ca|pac|i|ty² /kəpǽsɪti/

DESIGN AND PERFORMANCE

NOUN The **capacity** of a container such as a fuel tank is its volume, or the amount of liquid it can hold, measured in units such as quarts or gallons.

○ *The new model has increased fuel tank capacity, and will run for more than 150 miles between fill-ups.*

○ *This car has a fuel tank capacity of 9.9 gallons.*

car /kɑr/ (**cars**)

VEHICLE TYPES

NOUN A **car** is a motor vehicle with room for a small number of passengers.

○ *Her brakes failed and the car crashed into a shop front.*

○ *The plant manufactures pistons for car engines.*

car|bon mon|ox|ide (ABBR **CO**) /kɑrbən mənɒksaɪd/

FUELS, OILS, EMISSIONS, AND OTHER FLUIDS

NOUN **Carbon monoxide** is a poisonous gas that is produced especially by the engines of vehicles.

○ *The limit for carbon monoxide is 4.5 percent of the exhaust gas.*

○ *Catalytic converters reduce the amount of carbon monoxide in exhaust fumes.*

car|bu|re|tion /kɑrbəreɪʃⁿn/

VEHICLE COMPONENTS: ENGINE, TRANSMISSION, AND EXHAUST

NOUN **Carburetion** is the process of fuel becoming vapor and mixing with a stream of air in a carburetor.

○ The carburetion system has been refined to help the engine breathe better.

○ The purpose of carburetion is to provide a combustible mixture of fuel and air in the required quantity and quality for efficient operation of the engine under all conditions.

car|bu|re|tor /kɑrbəreɪtər/ (**carburetors**)

VEHICLE COMPONENTS: ENGINE, TRANSMISSION, AND EXHAUST

NOUN A **carburetor** is the part of an engine in which air and fuel are mixed together to form a vapor which can be burned.

○ The car has a new air induction system that forces outside air through the carburetor for better performance.

○ If the fuel line has blockages, the carburetor doesn't receive the correct amount of fuel and the motor runs poorly.

car|cass /kɑrkəs/ (**carcasss**)

VEHICLE COMPONENTS: BRAKES, STEERING, WHEELS, TIRES, AND SUSPENSION

NOUN The **carcass** is the structural body of a tire to which the rubber parts are fixed.

○ A layer of rubber covering the inside of the carcass of the tire had worn away.

○ The tread of the tire had worn through, and the white breaker-strip between tread and carcass had been exposed.

▶ SYNONYM:
casing

car|dan shaft /kɑrdæn ʃæft/ (**cardan shafts**)

VEHICLE COMPONENTS: ENGINE, TRANSMISSION, AND EXHAUST

NOUN A **cardan shaft** or **cardan drive** is a propeller shaft fitted with universal joints at each end.

○ A cardan shaft is the drive shaft between the gearbox and the back axle.

○ *Power is transmitted via cardan shafts to the final drives at the front ends of the forward and rear chassis.*

---

cast|er (BRIT **castor**) /kæstər/ (**casters**)

VEHICLE COMPONENTS: BRAKES, STEERING, WHEELS, TIRES, AND SUSPENSION

NOUN The **caster** is the amount by which a steered wheel trails behind the vertical axis about which it is steered.

○ *Positive caster projects the load of the vehicle to a point on the road ahead of the tire contact.*

○ *If the caster angle is too large, it will cause heavy steering and the driver will quickly get tired.*

▶ **COLLOCATIONS:**
  caster angle
  negative caster
  positive caster

---

cat|a|lyt|ic con|vert|er (ABBR **cat**) /kætəlɪtɪk kənvɜrtər/ (**catalytic converters**)

VEHICLE COMPONENTS: ENGINE, TRANSMISSION, AND EXHAUST

NOUN A **catalytic converter** is a device which is fitted to a car's exhaust to reduce the pollution coming from it.

○ *All models run on lead-free gasoline with a three-way catalytic converter.*

○ *Take account of fuel economy when choosing a new car, and, if possible, choose one with a catalytic converter to clean up the exhaust.*

Cat|er|pill|ar track /kætərpɪlər træk/ (**Caterpillar tracks**)

VEHICLE COMPONENTS: BRAKES, STEERING, WHEELS, TIRES, AND SUSPENSION

NOUN A **Caterpillar track** is a linked metal chain fastened around the wheels of a heavy vehicle to help it to move over rough ground. Caterpillar is a trademark.

○ *The Caterpillar track on the tractor has eight times the grip of round wheels.*

○ *Tractors with Caterpillar track on the wheels are known for their deep tillage, unequaled traction and drawbar pull, and low compaction.*

cen|tral lock|ing /sɛntrəl lɒkɪŋ/

VEHICLE COMPONENTS: BODYWORK, CONTROLS, AND ACCESSORIES

NOUN **Central locking** is a locking system in a vehicle by which all doors lock at the same time when the driver's door is locked.

○ The central locking system prevents individual doors remaining unlocked inadvertently.

○ A standard feature on all models is remote central locking for the doors.

ce|tane /siːteɪn/

FUELS, OILS, EMISSIONS, AND OTHER FLUIDS

NOUN **Cetane** is a colorless liquid hydrocarbon found in petroleum and used as the fuel on which the cetane number scale is based. It has a cetane number of 100.

○ It is highly desirable to have a high percentage of cetane, as it increases the efficiency of diesel engines.

○ The oil has higher cetane ratings, which is a measurement of the ignition quality of the fuel.

ce|tane num|ber /siːteɪn nʌmbər/

FUELS, OILS, EMISSIONS, AND OTHER FLUIDS

NOUN A **cetane number** is a measure of how long it takes fuel to ignite after injection. A high cetane number indicates a short lag.

○ The cetane number has an effect on the pollutants emitted by a direct-injection engine.

○ This diesel has a minimum cetane number of 51, up from 48, which could lead to a five percent reduction in diesel consumption.

chain and sprock|et drive /tʃeɪn ənd sprɒkɪt draɪv/ (**chain and sprocket drives**)

VEHICLE COMPONENTS: ENGINE, TRANSMISSION, AND EXHAUST

NOUN A **chain and sprocket drive** is a type of power transmission in which a roller chain engages with two or more toothed wheels or sprockets, used in engines as a drive from crankshaft to camshaft.

○ Chain and sprocket drives are the most common final drive system in motorcycles, a small front and larger rear toothed wheel linked by a roller chain.

○ A chain and sprocket drive is one way of conveying power to the wheels of a vehicle.

---

change-speed gear|box /tʃeɪndʒ spiːd ɡɪərbɒks/ (change-speed gearboxes)

VEHICLE COMPONENTS: ENGINE, TRANSMISSION, AND EXHAUST

NOUN A **change-speed gearbox** is a set of movable or constant gears which allows the speed ratio between input and output shafts to be changed either manually or automatically.

○ An overspeed facility is provided through a step-up change-speed gearbox.

○ A front-mounted engine drives the rear wheels through a shaft and differential, controlled through a friction clutch and change-speed gearbox.

---

charge¹ /tʃɑrdʒ/

VEHICLE COMPONENTS: LIGHTING AND ELECTRICAL/ELECTRONIC SYSTEMS

NOUN An electrical **charge** is an amount of electricity that is held in or carried by something such as a storage battery.

○ The battery was connected to charging leads overnight, and in the morning appeared to be full, but it didn't hold its charge.

○ There could be a problem with your battery, as there's no charge getting to your spark plugs.

---

charge² /tʃɑrdʒ/

VEHICLE COMPONENTS: ENGINE, TRANSMISSION, AND EXHAUST

NOUN The **charge** is the quantity of fuel (or air and fuel) that enters the cylinder of an engine on each stroke.

○ Sparks to fire the fuel charge in the cylinders are provided by a high tension magneto.

○ The greater the mass of the charge inducted, the higher the power produced.

chas|sis /tʃæsi/ (chassis)

VEHICLE COMPONENTS: BODYWORK, CONTROLS, AND ACCESSORIES

NOUN A **chassis** is the framework that a vehicle is built on.

○ A chassis is the supporting frame of a car, giving it strength and rigidity and helping to increase the car's crash resistance.

○ Generally large four-wheel drives are built on a separate chassis, much like a truck.

PRONUNCIATION

Note that you should not pronounce the "s" at the end of "chassis."

Note also the plural **chassis**, which is pronounced tʃæsiz.

---

chas|sis dy|na|mom|e|ter /tʃæsi daɪnəmɒmɪtər/ (chassis dynamometers)

VEHICLE TYPES

NOUN A **chassis dynamometer** is a piece of test equipment fitted with rollers for the wheels of a vehicle, that is capable of providing drive input and measuring output such as power and torque at the wheels.

○ The chassis dynamometer reproduces the load and inertia of the vehicle when driven on the road.

○ The chassis dynamometer measures the mechanical power of the vehicle at the drive-wheels.

---

choke /tʃoʊk/ (chokes)

VEHICLE COMPONENTS: BODYWORK, CONTROLS, AND ACCESSORIES

NOUN The **choke** in a vehicle is a device that reduces the amount of air going into the engine and makes it easier to start the engine or run it in cold weather.

○ A choke gets the engine firing right, with the right air/fuel mixture and lets it warm up without being too rich or too lean.

○ The choke circuit restricts the flow of air through the carburetor, thus increasing the percentage of fuel mixed with that air to help the engine start and warm up.

chro|mi|um /kroʊmiəm/

MATERIALS

NOUN **Chromium** is a hard, shiny, metallic element, used to make steel alloys and to coat other metals.

○ *The exterior bodywork is a mixture of stainless steel and chromium plating.*

○ *Chromium is commonly seen as reflective coatings on items like car bumpers.*

C|I en|gine (short for **compression ignition engine**)
/si aɪ ɛndʒɪn/ (**CI engines**)

VEHICLE COMPONENTS: ENGINE, TRANSMISSION, AND EXHAUST

NOUN A **CI engine** is an engine in which the fuel charge is ignited by the heat of compression.

○ *The process of combustion in the CI engine is fundamentally different from that in a spark-ignition engine.*

○ *In a CI engine, air is let into the combustion chamber and compressed to a very high pressure.*

cir|cuit break|er /sɜrkɪt breɪkər/ (**circuit breakers**)

VEHICLE COMPONENTS: LIGHTING AND ELECTRICAL/ELECTRONIC SYSTEMS

NOUN A **circuit breaker** is a device which can stop the flow of electricity around a circuit by switching itself off if anything goes wrong.

○ *There is always an internal circuit breaker to protect the instrument from overload.*

○ *The circuit breaker will open to stop current flow to the motor if motor temperature and current become too high.*

clear|ance vol|ume /klɪərəns vɒlyum/

VEHICLE COMPONENTS: ENGINE, TRANSMISSION, AND EXHAUST

NOUN The **clearance volume** is the volume remaining above the piston of an engine when it reaches top dead center.

○ *The maximum compression pressure in the piston is controlled by the clearance volume.*

○ *When the piston is at top dead center, the clearance volume is at a minimum. When the piston moves to bottom dead center, it is at a maximum.*

cli|mate con|trol /ˈklaɪmɪt kənˌtroʊl/

VEHICLE COMPONENTS: BODYWORK, CONTROLS, AND ACCESSORIES

NOUN **Climate control** is a system for controlling the temperature inside a vehicle.

○ The car's climate control system controls the heating and air-conditioning systems.

○ The climate control unit adjusts the temperature and air flow inside the car.

clutch /klʌtʃ/ (**clutches**)

VEHICLE COMPONENTS: ENGINE, TRANSMISSION, AND EXHAUST

NOUN The **clutch** in a vehicle is a mechanism which connects the engine with the gearbox to make the vehicle move, and disconnects them to allow a driver to change gear.

○ All manual transmissions require a clutch to engage or disengage the transmission.

○ Gradual engagement of the friction clutch allows the vehicle to move smoothly from stationary.

▶ COLLOCATIONS:
disengage the clutch
engage the clutch

> **CLUTCH PARTS INCLUDE:**
>
> bell housing, clutch disk, master cylinder
>
> The part of the car with which the driver operates the clutch is the **clutch pedal**.

clutch disk /klʌtʃ dɪsk/ (**clutch disks**)

VEHICLE COMPONENTS: ENGINE, TRANSMISSION, AND EXHAUST

NOUN The **clutch disk** or **clutch plate** is the rotating part of the clutch, to which the friction material is attached.

○ The clutch torque is generated by the friction of the friction material pads on each side of the clutch disk.

○ Equal pressure on each side of the clutch disk disengages the clutch, allowing normal operation of the torque converter.

clutch pe|dal /klʌtʃ pɛdᵊl/ (**clutch pedals**)

VEHICLE COMPONENTS: BODYWORK, CONTROLS, AND ACCESSORIES

NOUN The **clutch pedal** is the pedal by which the driver of a vehicle operates the clutch.

○ *In most models, the clutch pedal is on the left of the shaft, with the brake and throttle on the far right.*

○ *The engine turns off when the car is standing in neutral gear at a stoplight, but restarts instantly when you depress the clutch pedal and engage first gear.*

clutch slip /klʌtʃ slɪp/

VEHICLE COMPONENTS: ENGINE, TRANSMISSION, AND EXHAUST

NOUN **Clutch slip** is a faulty condition in which there is not enough friction in the clutch, so that engine speed rises without a corresponding increase in road speed.

○ *Excess oil on the clutch, or general wear and tear, can cause clutch slip.*

○ *Check for clutch slip, denoted by increasing high revs without a corresponding increase in speed.*

coach /koutʃ/ (**coaches**)

VEHICLE TYPES

NOUN A **coach** is a large, comfortable bus, usually single-deck, that carries passengers on long trips.

○ *This luxury coach can carry up to 24 people.*

○ *They are the market leader in bus and coach manufacture.*

coach|work /koutʃwɜrk/

VEHICLE COMPONENTS: BODYWORK, CONTROLS, AND ACCESSORIES

NOUN **Coachwork** is the paneled bodywork of a vehicle.

○ *The coachwork was available in a choice of 13 different polychromatic colors.*

○ *While the car was in the bodyshop for attention to the panels and paintwork, stress cracks in the coachwork were reinforced and welded.*

coil spring /kɔɪl sprɪŋ/ (coil springs)

VEHICLE COMPONENTS: ENGINE, TRANSMISSION, AND EXHAUST

NOUN A **coil spring** is a spiral-shaped spring that is used in suspensions or poppet valve mechanisms in vehicles.

○ The car has independent coil spring suspension.

○ Suspension is independent at the front with a new five-link and coil spring arrangement down the back.

col|umn shift /kɒləm ʃɪft/ (column shifts)

VEHICLE COMPONENTS: BODYWORK, CONTROLS, AND ACCESSORIES

NOUN A **column shift** is a gearshift lever mounted on the steering column.

○ The gearbox is automatic, and controlled by a column shift mounted in the side of the steering column.

○ On vehicles equipped with automatic transmission, you will have to disconnect the transmission shift rod from the steering column shift lever.

com|bus|tion cham|ber /kəmbʌstʃən tʃeɪmbər/ (combustion chambers)

VEHICLE COMPONENTS: ENGINE, TRANSMISSION, AND EXHAUST

NOUN The **combustion chamber** is the part of an engine in which combustion takes place.

○ The multi-point fuel injection system ensures that the right mix of air and fuel reach the combustion chamber of the engine.

○ Engineers have been working to optimize the way that the air moves as it enters the combustion chamber through two separate inlet valves.

com|mer|cial ve|hi|cle /kəmɜrʃºl viːɪkºl/ (commercial vehicles)

VEHICLE TYPES

NOUN A **commercial vehicle** is a vehicle that is licensed to be used for the transportation of goods or materials rather than passengers.

○ Light to medium-sized commercial vehicles are used to transport relatively light goods.

○ *Thanks to its load carrying capacity, a five-seater one-tonne double cab is counted for tax purposes as a commercial vehicle.*

---

com|pres|sion¹ /kəmprɛʃ°n/ (compressions)

VEHICLE COMPONENTS: ENGINE, TRANSMISSION, AND EXHAUST

NOUN **Compression** is the increase of pressure in an engine cylinder as the piston travels toward top dead center.

○ *Without a lubricant, the fuel can cause the valve seats and valve guides to burn away and you will lose compression and power.*

○ *Some of the effective compression of the engine is lost due to an open valve.*

---

com|pres|sion² /kəmprɛʃ°n/

DESIGN AND PERFORMANCE

NOUN **Compression** of a solid material involves applying forces that reduce the distance between the points of load.

○ *The coil spring is in compression when under a load.*

○ *Too much compression and the part will shatter into many pieces.*

▶ **COLLOCATION:**
   in compression

---

com|pres|sion ra|ti|o /kəmprɛʃ°n reɪʃoʊ/ (compression ratios)

VEHICLE COMPONENTS: ENGINE, TRANSMISSION, AND EXHAUST

NOUN The **compression ratio** in an engine is the ratio of the volume of the cylinder plus combustion chamber at the bottom of the stroke (when the volume is greatest) to the volume at the top of the stroke (when the volume is least).

○ *This design has the facility to tilt the cylinder head slightly, so that the compression ratio can be altered automatically according to engine load and revs.*

○ *Not all engines have the same compression ratio, and an engine with a ratio set for a 95RON fuel will usually gain no benefit from using 98RON fuel since the pistons will not compress the fuel to its maximum.*

com|pres|sion stroke /kəmprɛʃ°n stroʊk/ (**compression strokes**)

VEHICLE COMPONENTS: ENGINE, TRANSMISSION, AND EXHAUST

NOUN The **compression stroke** is the stroke in an engine in which the air or air/fuel mixture is compressed before ignition.

○ *The intake valve closes and the piston starts up on the compression stroke.*

○ *During the compression stroke, the piston moves up the cylinder, squeezing the fuel-air mix.*

con|nect|ing rod (ABBR **con rod**) /kənɛktɪŋ rɒd/ (**connecting rods**)

VEHICLE COMPONENTS: ENGINE, TRANSMISSION, AND EXHAUST

NOUN A **connecting rod** is a rod that connects the crank to the piston in an engine.

○ *The connecting rods connect the piston to the crankshaft.*

○ *The hot, expanding gases of combustion push on the piston, which moves a connecting rod, which turns a crankshaft.*

RELATED WORDS

The following also connect parts of vehicles:

beam axle
connects the nearside wheel to the offside wheel

exhaust manifold
connects the engine to the exhaust pipe

track rod
connects the steering arms of steered wheels

---

con|stant mesh gear|box /kɒnstənt mɛʃ gɪərbɒks/ (**constant mesh gearboxes**)

VEHICLE COMPONENTS: ENGINE, TRANSMISSION, AND EXHAUST

NOUN A **constant mesh gearbox** is a type of transmission in which all forward gear pairs remain engaged.

○ *In a constant mesh gearbox, all gears are in mesh all the time.*

○ *The constant mesh gearbox is a type of manual transmission in which the gears are meshed or fixed to their positions.*

con|stant ve|loc|i|ty joint (ABBR **CV joint**) /kɒnstənt vəlɒsɪti dʒɔɪnt/ (**constant velocity joints**)

VEHICLE COMPONENTS: ENGINE, TRANSMISSION, AND EXHAUST

NOUN A **constant velocity joint** is a universal joint in which the output shaft rotates at constant speed if the input shaft speed is constant.

○ *The rattling in the engine may mean that the constant velocity joint part of the drive train is worn.*

○ *Whatever the operating angle of the constant velocity joint, the rotational speed of the output shaft is the same as that of the input shaft.*

con|tact break|er /kɒntækt breɪkər/ (**contact breakers**)

VEHICLE COMPONENTS: LIGHTING AND ELECTRICAL/ELECTRONIC SYSTEMS

NOUN A **contact breaker** is a mechanical switch, activated by a rotating cam, that makes or breaks the ignition circuit to send a spark to the spark plug.

○ *The contact breaker is a mechanical device in the distributor system and is used to break the circuit.*

○ *When the primary circuit is broken the current tends to continue flowing and a spark jumps across the separated contact breaker points.*

con|vert|i|ble /kənvɜrtɪbəl/ (**convertibles**)

VEHICLE TYPES

NOUN A **convertible** is a car with a soft roof that can be folded down or removed.

○ *The top can be folded down easily in this convertible.*

○ *The soft roof of the convertible can be removed easily.*

cool|ant /kulənt/ (**coolants**)

FUELS, OILS, EMISSIONS, AND OTHER FLUIDS

NOUN **Coolant** is a liquid used to keep an engine, compressor, or other machine cool while it is operating.

○ *Keep your engine oil topped up: remember it acts as a coolant as well as a lubricant.*

○ *Engineers have also improved the engine's cooling passages to increase coolant flow.*

---

cool|ing sys|tem /kulɪŋ sɪstəm/ (cooling systems)

VEHICLE COMPONENTS: ENGINE, TRANSMISSION, AND EXHAUST

NOUN An engine's **cooling system** is a set of parts designed to make it less hot while it is in operation.

○ *The cooling system is quite conventional with a block-mounted, belt-driven water pump circulating 25 pints of water.*

○ *Engine cooling systems rarely come under greater stress than when sitting still in heavy traffic with no airflow over the radiator.*

---

coun|ter shaft /kaʊntər ʃæft/ (counter shafts)

VEHICLE COMPONENTS: ENGINE, TRANSMISSION, AND EXHAUST

NOUN A **counter shaft** is a shaft that runs parallel to the main shaft in a gearbox, and carries the pinion wheels.

○ *In a normal sliding gear transmission there are two shafts, a main shaft and a counter shaft.*

○ *A counter shaft is a manual transmission shaft driven by the clutch shaft and its input gear.*

▶ **SYNONYM:**
cluster gear

---

cou|pling¹ /kʌplɪŋ/ (couplings)

VEHICLE COMPONENTS: ENGINE, TRANSMISSION, AND EXHAUST

NOUN A **coupling** is a device which is used to join two pieces of equipment, such as rotating shafts, together.

○ *A coupling connects the two rotating shafts.*

○ *The coupling provides a connection between two adjacent rotating shafts that can easily be broken and restored.*

cou|pling² /kʌplɪŋ/ (couplings)

VEHICLE COMPONENTS: BODYWORK, CONTROLS, AND ACCESSORIES

NOUN A **coupling** is a device which is used to join two vehicles together.

○ *Before driving away, re-check the trailer coupling.*

○ *Brakes must be checked before towing, and all fittings, couplings, and safety chains need to be securely fastened.*

cour|te|sy light /kɜrtɪsi laɪt/ (courtesy lights)

VEHICLE COMPONENTS: BODYWORK, CONTROLS, AND ACCESSORIES

NOUN A **courtesy light** is an interior light in a vehicle that goes on when the door is opened.

○ *She was sitting in the car studying a map by the courtesy light.*

○ *The white portion of the light serves as a courtesy light when getting in or out of the car. The red portion serves as a marker light to oncoming traffic that the door is open.*

crank /kræŋk/ (cranks)

VEHICLE COMPONENTS: ENGINE, TRANSMISSION, AND EXHAUST

NOUN A **crank** is an arm attached to a shaft that carries a handle or pedal parallel to the shaft.

○ *One of the simplest of mechanical inventions was a crank which turns a shaft.*

○ *The connecting rod connects the crank to the piston.*

crank|case /kræŋkkeɪs/ (crankcases)

VEHICLE COMPONENTS: ENGINE, TRANSMISSION, AND EXHAUST

NOUN A **crankcase** is the part of an engine that contains and supports the crankshaft and main bearings.

○ *The main hood vent, located under the headlamp, channels fresh air to the crankcase.*

○ *The engineer removed the crankcase to expose the crankshaft end bearings.*

crank|case com|pres|sion /ˈkræŋkkeɪs kəmˈprɛʃ°n/

VEHICLE COMPONENTS: ENGINE, TRANSMISSION, AND EXHAUST

NOUN **Crankcase compression** is the method of starting some smaller two-stroke engines, where the mixture charge is compressed in a sealed crankcase by the descending piston before passing to the combustion chamber.

○ *In two-stroke cycle engines using crankcase compression, lubricating oil must be added to the inlet air.*

○ *The two-stroke cycle uses crankcase compression to pump the fresh charge into the cylinder.*

crank|pin /ˈkræŋkpɪn/ (**crankpins**)

VEHICLE COMPONENTS: ENGINE, TRANSMISSION, AND EXHAUST

NOUN A **crankpin** is the part of the crank of a crankshaft to which the connecting rod is attached.

○ *Crankpins transfer up-and-down motion between the crankshaft and connecting rod.*

○ *The big end of the connecting rod is connected to the crankpin of the crankshaft by way of a bearing.*

crank|shaft /ˈkræŋkʃæft/ (**crankshafts**)

VEHICLE COMPONENTS: ENGINE, TRANSMISSION, AND EXHAUST

NOUN A **crankshaft** is the main shaft of an internal combustion engine.

○ *Crankshafts usually have one crank for each cylinder.*

○ *The crankshaft was reground and fitted with new main bearings.*

crank|shaft end bear|ing /ˈkræŋkʃæft ɛnd ˈbɛərɪŋ/ (**crankshaft end bearings**)

VEHICLE COMPONENTS: ENGINE, TRANSMISSION, AND EXHAUST

NOUN The **crankshaft end bearing** is the bearing between the connecting rod and the crankshaft of an internal combustion engine.

○ *The seal below the flywheel was leaking because of a worn crankshaft end bearing.*

> ○ *They discovered that the knocking sound in the engine was due to the failure of one of the crankshaft end bearings.*

---

crew cab /kruː kæb/ (**crew cabs**)

VEHICLE COMPONENTS: BODYWORK, CONTROLS, AND ACCESSORIES

NOUN A **crew cab** is a cab in a vehicle such as a fire engine that has been extended with a second row of seats to carry additional crew.

> ○ *This vehicle comes in regular cab, extended cab and crew cab models.*

> ○ *The crew cab of the truck offers seating for five or six, and generous legroom.*

---

crude oil /kruːd ɔɪl/

FUELS, OILS, EMISSIONS, AND OTHER FLUIDS

NOUN **Crude oil** is oil in its natural state before it has been processed or refined.

> ○ *The refining of crude oil to produce petroleum generates a range of by-products.*

> ○ *The Braer tanker disaster spilled 84,500 tonnes of crude oil off Shetland in 1993.*

---

cruise con|trol /kruːz kəntroʊl/

VEHICLE COMPONENTS: BODYWORK, CONTROLS, AND ACCESSORIES

NOUN **Cruise control** is an electronic control system in a vehicle that automatically keeps the vehicle's speed at the same level.

> ○ *I set the cruise control at the 55-mile-an-hour speed limit.*

> ○ *On the freeway, she set the cruise control at a legal 70mph and sat back in her seat.*

---

crush zone /krʌʃ zoʊn/ (**crush zones**)

VEHICLE COMPONENTS: BODYWORK, CONTROLS, AND ACCESSORIES

NOUN The **crush zone** is the part of a vehicle's bodywork that is designed to absorb the energy in a crash, reducing the amount that is felt by passengers inside the vehicle.

> ○ *SUVs have less of a front-end crush zone to absorb impact, causing the air bags to deploy with more force.*

○ *When a fuel tank is located within a vehicle's crush zone, it is very likely that the tank will rupture during an impact.*

▶ **SYNONYM:**
crumple zone

---

cut-out[1] /kʌt aʊt/ (**cut-outs**)

VEHICLE COMPONENTS: ENGINE, TRANSMISSION, AND EXHAUST

NOUN A **cut-out** is any device that stops a mechanical unit or electrical circuit from operating.

○ *All heaters have an automatic safety cut-out that switches the heater off if the air grilles are accidentally covered.*

○ *For extra security, fit an alarm, immobilizer, or engine cut-out device.*

---

cut-out[2] /kʌt aʊt/ (**cut-outs**)

VEHICLE COMPONENTS: LIGHTING AND ELECTRICAL/ELECTRONIC SYSTEMS

NOUN A **cut-out** is a switch in a control box that stops the current flow from returning to a dynamo when the battery capacity is greater than the voltage of the dynamo.

○ *The battery cut-out switch was located in the passenger footwell.*

○ *As the voltage rises, the cut-out connects the dynamo to charge the battery.*

---

cyl|in|der /sɪlɪndər/ (**cylinders**)

VEHICLE COMPONENTS: ENGINE, TRANSMISSION, AND EXHAUST

NOUN In an engine, a **cylinder** is a part with flat circular ends and long straight sides in which a piston moves backward and forward.

○ *The carburetor heats the gas before it enters the engine cylinder.*

○ *Both engines feature four valves per cylinder and a host of engineering improvements.*

cyl|in|der block /sɪlɪndər blɒk/ (**cylinder blocks**)

VEHICLE COMPONENTS: ENGINE, TRANSMISSION, AND EXHAUST

NOUN A **cylinder block** is the part of an engine containing the cylinders.

○ *The cylinder block acts as the central frame of the engine and all the other engine components are attached to it.*

○ *The 2.4-liter engine has been extensively modified, with a redesigned cylinder block, cylinder head, and crankshaft.*

cyl|in|der head /sɪlɪndər hɛd/ (**cylinder heads**)

VEHICLE COMPONENTS: ENGINE, TRANSMISSION, AND EXHAUST

NOUN A **cylinder head** is the part of an engine that closes the upper ends of the cylinders.

○ *When I removed the cylinder head, I found the tops of the pistons and inlet valves covered in a shiny substance.*

○ *The cylinder head is an intricate casting mated to the top of the cylinder block.*

cyl|in|der lin|er /sɪlɪndər laɪnər/ (**cylinder liners**)

VEHICLE COMPONENTS: ENGINE, TRANSMISSION, AND EXHAUST

NOUN A **cylinder liner** is a thin-walled hard metal cylinder inserted into a cylinder block of an engine and in which the piston runs.

○ *There were also signs of leakage on the cylinder liner seals of two of the cylinders.*

○ *A head-cooled cylinder liner has bores for coolant flow in the head of the cylinder wall that protrudes out of the crankcase.*

Dd

damp|er /dǽmpər/ (dampers)

NOUN A **damper** is a device for reducing vibration in an engine, camshaft drive, or vehicle suspension.

- ○ *A vibration damper is fitted to the front end of the crankshaft to minimize vibrations.*
- ○ *The damper is designed with the aim of absorbing vibration energy and dissipating it as heat.*

dash|board (ABBR dash) /dǽʃbɔrd/ (dashboards)

NOUN The **dashboard** in a vehicle is the panel facing the driver's seat where most of the instruments and switches are.

- ○ *An automobile dashboard monitors vehicle speed, engine speed, and engine temperature.*
- ○ *The dashboard in a car provides critical information needed to operate the vehicle at a glance, indicating speed, temperature, oil pressure, and revolutions per minute.*

dead cen|ter /dɛd sɛntər/ (dead centers)

NOUN The **dead center** is the position of an engine's piston when it is at the very top or bottom of its stroke.

- ○ *The maximum travel of the piston between the two dead centers is the stroke.*
- ○ *A small crank-throw reduces both the crankshaft turning-effort and the distance the piston moves between the dead centers.*

det|o|na|tion /dɛtˀneɪʃˀn/

NOUN **Detonation** is rapid and uncontrolled combustion, especially in the cylinder of a spark ignition engine which is operating with a fuel with inadequate octane.

○ Combustion chamber contours can be blended slightly to reduce the tendency to detonation.

○ Detonation can cause the temperatures inside the cylinder head to rise to the melting point of the components inside it, with the piston usually going first.

di|ag|nos|tic test|ing /daɪəgnɒstɪk tɛstɪŋ/

NOUN **Diagnostic testing** is the testing of a vehicle, or one of its systems or parts, in order to identify why it is not working properly.

○ A facility offering diagnostic testing will give you specific information about how well the carburetor, battery, alternator, etc, are functioning.

○ Diagnostic testing showed that the engine produced less power than expected because the ignition timing was too retarded.

di|a|phragm /daɪəfræm/ (**diaphragms**)

NOUN A **diaphragm** is a flexible disk or membrane which moves under pressure and causes a rod in a brake or carburetor to move.

○ When engine vacuum is high, the diaphragm is depressed more, which opens the valve more, letting more fuel back into the fuel tank.

○ A flexible diaphragm regulates the amount of fuel available inside the carburetor.

die|sel cy|cle /diːzˀl saɪkˀl/ (**diesel cycles**)

NOUN The **diesel cycle** is the cycle of an internal combustion engine in which air is compressed, heat is added at constant pressure by injecting fuel, the mixture is expanded to do work on the piston, and then the combustion products are removed by the exhaust.

○ *During the suction stroke in a diesel cycle, engine air is sucked inside the cylinder.*

○ *In a diesel cycle, the fuel and air are compressed separately and brought together at the time of combustion.*

---

dif|fer|en|tial /dɪfərɛnʃ°l/ (differentials)

VEHICLE COMPONENTS: ENGINE, TRANSMISSION, AND EXHAUST

NOUN A **differential** is a system of gears in a vehicle which allows two shafts to rotate at different speeds.

○ *The five-speed manual transmission channels the power to a limited-slip differential.*

○ *The differential enables the vehicle's rear wheels to revolve at different speeds in rounding corners.*

---

di|lu|tion /daɪluʃ°n/ (dilutions)

FUELS, OILS, EMISSIONS, AND OTHER FLUIDS

NOUN A **dilution** is a liquid that has been diluted with water or another liquid, so that it becomes weaker.

○ *Engines in good mechanical condition will usually show a small amount of fuel dilution in the used engine oil.*

○ *Even engines in good mechanical condition will sometimes show a small amount of oil dilution in the sump.*

---

dim|mer switch (In BRIT use **dip switch**) /dɪmər swɪtʃ/ (dimmer switches)

VEHICLE COMPONENTS: LIGHTING AND ELECTRICAL/ELECTRONIC SYSTEMS

NOUN A **dimmer switch** is an electrical switch which turns off the full beam of a headlamp and turns on the low beam.

○ *Controls on the panel to the driver's left are for emergency flasher and headlamp dimmer switch.*

○ *A dimmer switch is used for changing headlamps from high beam to low beam.*

di|rect in|jec|tion /dɪrɛkt ɪndʒɛkʃ°n/

VEHICLE COMPONENTS: ENGINE, TRANSMISSION, AND EXHAUST

NOUN **Direct injection** is a diesel engine injection system in which the fuel is injected directly into the engine cylinder.

○ *Direct injection diesel engines will often start from cold with relative ease.*

○ *With direct injection, the fuel enters the cylinder late in the compression stroke.*

disk brake /dɪsk breɪk/ (**disk brakes**)

VEHICLE COMPONENTS: BRAKES, STEERING, WHEELS, TIRES, AND SUSPENSION

NOUN A **disk brake** is a brake in which external friction pads press onto a disk, usually by the action of a caliper.

○ *Disk brakes have one, two or four hydraulically driven pistons that force pads against revolving rotors.*

○ *The most common disk brake parts to wear, by design, are the brake pads.*

dis|place|ment /dɪspleɪsmənt/

VEHICLE COMPONENTS: ENGINE, TRANSMISSION, AND EXHAUST

NOUN **Displacement** is the volume of air/fuel mixture that can be taken into an engine's cylinder with each induction stroke, multiplied by the number of cylinders.

○ *A cylinder's displacement is the volume of the cylinder when the piston is at bottom dead center.*

○ *The four-cylinder engine provides amazing power for its displacement and returns impressive fuel economy as well.*

dis|trib|u|tor /dɪstrɪbyətər/ (**distributors**)

VEHICLE COMPONENTS: ENGINE, TRANSMISSION, AND EXHAUST

NOUN A **distributor** is an engine-driven switch that sends the high-voltage ignition current to each spark plug in turn.

○ *We adjusted the distributor with each run, to tune the engine to its peak.*

○ *The coil wire conducts the high voltage to the distributor, where the cap and rotor distribute it to the appropriate spark plug.*

D

> **WORD BUILDER**
> **-or** = performing
>
> The suffix **-or** is often used to form words connected with performing a particular function: **accelerator**, **alternator**, **governor**, **indicator**, **injector**.

D-post /diˈpoʊst/ (**D-posts**)

VEHICLE COMPONENTS: BODYWORK, CONTROLS, AND ACCESSORIES

NOUN A **D-post** is part of the bodywork of a vehicle that supports the roof and against which the rear door closes.

○ D-posts are only found on four- or five-door cars.

○ The uninterrupted lines of the rear glass area conceal the D-posts (roof supports).

---

drag /dræg/

DESIGN AND PERFORMANCE

NOUN **Drag** is used to describe the forces in the air that push against the movement of a vehicle.

○ With less drag, a car can accelerate faster, especially at higher speeds, because it needs less horsepower to move.

○ If your brakes aren't properly adjusted, they can create drag on your car and waste lots of gasoline.

---

drain plug /dreɪn plʌg/ (**drain plugs**)

VEHICLE COMPONENTS: ENGINE, TRANSMISSION, AND EXHAUST

NOUN A **drain plug** is a plug which is taken out to allow a fluid to be drained from a tank such as an engine oil pan or sump.

○ Remove the oil drain plug, and allow oil to drain out.

○ Remove the drain plug under the engine with the wrench, and let the oil flow into the pan.

draw|bar /drɔbɑr/ (drawbars)

VEHICLE COMPONENTS: BODYWORK, CONTROLS, AND ACCESSORIES

NOUN A **drawbar** is a rigid bar or frame by which a full trailer is towed and steered.

○ *The caravan should be loaded so that most of the weight is over the drawbar.*

○ *An agricultural machine comprises a body and a drawbar, which allows the machine to be moved along during work and during transport.*

drive shaft /draɪv ʃæft/ (drive shafts)

VEHICLE COMPONENTS: ENGINE, TRANSMISSION, AND EXHAUST

NOUN A **drive shaft** is a shaft in a vehicle that transfers power from the gearbox to the wheels.

○ *The coupling of the drive shaft to the gearbox allows for the movement of the axles.*

○ *Power from the engine is delivered to the transmission, which in turn delivers power to the drive shaft, which in turn transmits power to the drive wheels.*

drive train /draɪv treɪn/ (drive trains)

VEHICLE COMPONENTS: ENGINE, TRANSMISSION, AND EXHAUST

NOUN A **drive train** is a system including all the parts linking the engine of a vehicle to the wheels.

○ *Each spark plug operates in a continuing process that puts power into the drive train and propels the car.*

○ *The drive train of a vehicle is formed by the components that are responsible for transferring power to the drive wheels.*

drum brake /drʌm breɪk/ (drum brakes)

VEHICLE COMPONENTS: BRAKES, STEERING, WHEELS, TIRES, AND SUSPENSION

NOUN A **drum brake** is a brake in which a brake shoe presses against a drum or a closed cylinder attached to a vehicle wheel.

○ *A drum brake is a brake in which the friction is caused by a set of shoes that press against a rotating drum-shaped surface.*

○ *The wheel components in a drum brake system are the wheel cylinder, drum, shoes, adjuster, and mounting hardware.*

---

dwell an|gle /dwɛl æŋgᵊl/ (**dwell angles**)

VEHICLE COMPONENTS: ENGINE, TRANSMISSION, AND EXHAUST

NOUN **Dwell angle** is the amount of time, measured as degrees of rotation, that contact breakers close in a distributor.

○ *Unless dwell angle is accurate, ignition timing won't be accurate.*

○ *The period, measured in degree of cam rotation, during which the contact points remain closed is called the dwell angle.*

Ee

ec|cen|tric¹ /ɪksɛntrɪk/ (eccentrics)

VEHICLE COMPONENTS: ENGINE, TRANSMISSION, AND EXHAUST

NOUN An **eccentric** is any circular component of a vehicle that rotates around an off-center axis.

- ○ *The slide valves were worked by eccentrics, rods, and rocking links.*
- ○ *When the eccentric rotates, the rocker arm moves the diaphragm up and down.*

ec|cen|tric² /ɪksɛntrɪk/

DESIGN AND PERFORMANCE

ADJECTIVE An **eccentric** component of a vehicle rotates around an off-center axis.

- ○ *Tapping screw heads should not be eccentric with the axis of the screw by more than 3 percent of the maximum head diameter.*
- ○ *The action of the eccentric cam moves the diaphragm up and down, pumping fuel to the engine.*

  ▶ COLLOCATION:
  eccentric cam

e|las|to|mer /ɪlæstəmər/

MATERIALS

NOUN **Elastomer** is a material, usually a synthetic rubber or plastic, that has elastic mechanical properties.

- ○ *The shock absorber is made of an elastomer rubber.*
- ○ *The high resilience, low heat build-up, and excellent dynamic properties of elastomer make it an ideal rubber for automotive tires.*

e|lec|tric re|tard|er /ɪlɛktrɪk rɪtɑrdər/ (**electric retarders**)

VEHICLE COMPONENTS: BRAKES, STEERING, WHEELS, TIRES, AND SUSPENSION

NOUN An **electric retarder** is an electromagnetic transmission brake that is only effective when a vehicle is moving.

○ *There are conventional shoe brakes on all wheels of tractor and trailer, plus an electric retarder mounted on the drive shaft of the tractor and on a live axle of the trailer.*

○ *You will need to specify electric retarders to meet the regulations for use in such hilly terrain.*

e|lec|tric ve|hi|cle (ABBR **EV**) /ɪlɛktrɪk viɪkᵊl/ (**electric vehicles**)

VEHICLE TYPES

NOUN An **electric vehicle** is a vehicle that is driven by an electric motor which draws its current either from storage batteries or from overhead cables.

○ *A fuel-cell car is an electric vehicle that makes its own electricity.*

○ *The restricted range of the electric vehicle can be a disadvantage in the countryside.*

e|lec|tron|ic sta|bil|i|ty con|trol sys|tem
/ɪlɛktrɒnɪk stəbɪlɪti kəntroʊl sɪstəm/ (**electronic stability control systems**)

VEHICLE COMPONENTS: BODYWORK, CONTROLS, AND ACCESSORIES

NOUN An **electronic stability control system** is an electronic system designed to stop a driver from losing control of steering by engaging the brakes or reducing or increasing power to individual wheels.

○ *All vehicles come equipped with an electronic stability control system that can detect skidding or loss of steering control.*

○ *The all-wheel drive system is modulated by a specially calibrated electronic stability control system, that is designed to keep the car on the road.*

el|lip|ti|cal spring /ɪlɪptɪkᵊl sprɪŋ/ (**elliptical springs**)

VEHICLE COMPONENTS: BRAKES, STEERING, WHEELS, TIRES, AND SUSPENSION

NOUN An **elliptical spring** is a spring that is made from two springs in the shape of elongated ovals laid cut in half and back-to-back.

○ An elliptical spring is securely clamped at each end to the axle.

○ The tractor-trailer has an elliptical spring suspension system.

e

e|mis|sion /ɪmɪʃᵊn/ (**emissions**)

FUELS, OILS, EMISSIONS, AND OTHER FLUIDS

NOUN An **emission of** something such as gas or vapor is the release of it into the atmosphere.

○ The emission of gases such as carbon dioxide should be stabilized at their present level.

○ Transport causes emission of carbon dioxide which in turn causes global climate changes.

end float /ɛnd floʊt/

VEHICLE COMPONENTS: ENGINE, TRANSMISSION, AND EXHAUST

NOUN **End float** is the amount by which a shaft can move lengthwise.

○ The lubricated grooves allow the hubs to shift if shafts are misaligned or subject to end float.

○ The right amount of end float is important so that your axle does not overload the opposite hub bearing by feeding axle loads from one side of the car to the opposite bearing.

en|gage /ɪngeɪdʒ/ (**engages, engaged, engaging**)

VEHICLE COMPONENTS: ENGINE, TRANSMISSION, AND EXHAUST

VERB If you **engage** a clutch or a gear, you put the mechanism into operation.

○ She engaged the clutch and the vehicle started to move away.

○ Starting up the engine, he engaged first gear and began to turn the car.

▶ COLLOCATION:
engage the clutch

en|gine /ɛndʒɪn/ (engines)

VEHICLE COMPONENTS: ENGINE, TRANSMISSION, AND EXHAUST

NOUN The **engine** of a vehicle is the part that converts the energy of the fuel into mechanical energy, and produces the power which makes the vehicle move.

○ He got into the driving seat and started the engine.

○ He was sitting in the driver's seat revving the engine to clean out the carburetor.

en|gine bay /ɛndʒɪn beɪ/ (engine bays)

VEHICLE COMPONENTS: ENGINE, TRANSMISSION, AND EXHAUST

NOUN The **engine bay** is the space inside a vehicle for the engine.

○ Corrosion in the engine bay was caused by both water and brake fluid leaks.

○ Wiring is easily accessible and the fuel tank is reached through the engine bay.

en|gine man|age|ment sys|tem (ABBR **EMS**) /ɛndʒɪn mænɪdʒmənt sɪstəm/ (engine management systems)

VEHICLE COMPONENTS: BODYWORK, CONTROLS, AND ACCESSORIES

NOUN The **engine management system** is the arrangement of the devices for controlling a vehicle's engine.

○ If the car is stolen, the unit will block the vehicle's engine management system and prevent the engine being restarted.

○ The engine management system shuts down four of the eight cylinders when the power isn't needed.

en|gine mount /ɛndʒɪn maʊnt/ (engine mounts)

VEHICLE COMPONENTS: ENGINE, TRANSMISSION, AND EXHAUST

NOUN The **engine mount** is the part of the chassis on which an engine is supported.

○ The vibration may be due to an overly worn or defective engine mount.

○ Engine mounts are used to connect a car engine to the car frame.

en|rich|ment /ɪnrɪtʃmənt/

FUELS, OILS, EMISSIONS, AND OTHER FLUIDS

NOUN **Enrichment** is the process of increasing the proportion of fuel to air in a carburetor.

○ *Excessive enrichment of the air-fuel mixture will result in a substantial loss of power.*

○ *The choke is a fuel enrichment mechanism in a carburetor.*

er|go|nom|ic /ɜːgənɒmɪk/

VEHICLE COMPONENTS: BODYWORK, CONTROLS, AND ACCESSORIES

ADJECTIVE **Ergonomic** equipment or parts in a vehicle are designed to be comfortable or efficient for a passenger or driver.

○ *The ergonomic design of the driver space meant that I could not reach or use the brake pedal.*

○ *The review praised the car's ergonomic design for excellent comfort and efficiency.*

▶ COLLOCATION:
  ergonomic design

er|go|nom|ics /ɜːgənɒmɪks/

DESIGN AND PERFORMANCE

NOUN **Ergonomics** is the study of how equipment and parts in a vehicle can be arranged in the most efficient and comfortable way.

○ *Ergonomics is important in primary safety, preventing accidents from occurring, and in the everyday comfortable and convenient use of vehicles.*

○ *The car's interior was designed without much scientific attention to ergonomics, and it was not very comfortable to drive.*

ex|haust a|nal|y|sis /ɪgzɔːst ənælɪsɪs/ (**exhaust analyses**)

FUELS, OILS, EMISSIONS, AND OTHER FLUIDS

NOUN An **exhaust analysis** is an examination of the constituents of an engine's gases, vapors, and particulates.

○ Information from an exhaust analysis can be used to diagnose incorrect air-fuel mixtures.

○ Dynamometer test results show exhaust analysis done before and after the converter has been fitted.

---

ex|haust e|mis|sions /ɪgzɔːst imɪʃᵊns/

FUELS, OILS, EMISSIONS, AND OTHER FLUIDS

NOUN Exhaust emissions are substances that come out of an exhaust system into the atmosphere.

○ A high-capacity catalytic converter reduces the level of harmful exhaust emissions discharged into the atmosphere.

○ Hybrid-electric vehicles cut pollution and comply with laws limiting vehicle exhaust emissions.

---

ex|haust gas re|cir|cul|a|tion (ABBR EGR) /ɪgzɔːst gæs risɜːrkyəleɪʃᵊn/

VEHICLE COMPONENTS: ENGINE, TRANSMISSION, AND EXHAUST

NOUN Exhaust gas recirculation is the process of mixing exhaust gas with air taken in to make sure that all fuel is burned before entering the atmosphere.

○ The exhaust gas recirculation system helps to keep the emissions of the manual transmission model below the 150g/km level.

○ Exhaust gas recirculation involves recirculating a controllable proportion of the engine's exhaust back into the intake air.

---

ex|haust man|i|fold /ɪgzɔːst mænɪfoʊld/ (exhaust manifolds)

VEHICLE COMPONENTS: ENGINE, TRANSMISSION, AND EXHAUST

NOUN An **exhaust manifold** is a heat-resistant tube that connects an engine to an exhaust pipe.

○ The exhaust manifold collects the exhaust gases from a number of cylinders and leads them to the exhaust pipe.

○ The exhaust manifold is the first in a series of pipes encountered by the exhaust gases after combustion.

ex|haust pipe /ɪgzɔst paɪp/ (**exhaust pipes**)

VEHICLE COMPONENTS: ENGINE, TRANSMISSION, AND EXHAUST

NOUN The **exhaust pipe** is the pipe that carries the gas out of the engine of a vehicle.

○ *When you start your car, a little gasoline gets turned into a mixture of gases and soot that come out of the exhaust pipe.*

○ *There should be no smoke from the exhaust pipe even if the engine is worked hard.*

> **THE EXHAUST SYSTEM INCLUDES:**
>
> catalytic converter, exhaust manifold, exhaust pipe, exhaust valve, muffler, particulate filter, turbocharger

ex|haust valve /ɪgzɔst vælv/ (**exhaust valves**)

VEHICLE COMPONENTS: ENGINE, TRANSMISSION, AND EXHAUST

NOUN An **exhaust valve** is a valve that releases burned gases from a cylinder.

○ *The exhaust valve closes during the initial part of the induction stroke.*

○ *The inlet valve usually opens a little before top dead center and the exhaust valve remains open a little after top dead center.*

ex|plo|sion /ɪksploʊʒ³n/ (**explosions**)

FUELS, OILS, EMISSIONS, AND OTHER FLUIDS

NOUN An **explosion** is a very rapid combustion, with a sudden loud noise, that is damaging to internal combustion engines.

○ *Ignition of unburned residual mixture is not likely to be the cause of an explosion in an engine cylinder.*

○ *Excessive heating of the fuel, due to gasoline pipes being too near the engine, was the cause of the explosion.*

eye[1] /aɪ/ (**eyes**)

VEHICLE COMPONENTS: BODYWORK, CONTROLS, AND ACCESSORIES

NOUN An **eye** is the end of a link which has a flat part with a hole by which it can be attached.

○ *Place the eye over the stud and secure with a nut.*

○ *A linkage consisting of an eye end and fork end is stronger because the pivot pin is in double rather than single shear.*

---

eye² /aɪ/ (eyes)

E

VEHICLE COMPONENTS: BRAKES, STEERING, WHEELS, TIRES, AND SUSPENSION

NOUN An **eye** is the end of a leaf spring by which it is attached to a vehicle.

○ *Extending the frame allowed the rear spring front eye to join the chassis assembly.*

○ *He connected the eye of the leaf spring to the vehicle's chassis.*

Ff

fair|ing /fɛərɪŋ/

VEHICLE COMPONENTS: BODYWORK, CONTROLS, AND ACCESSORIES

NOUN **Fairing** is any panel on a vehicle's bodywork that joins other panels with a smooth curve.

- ○ *The bodywork on the car was very streamlined, with side fairings between and behind the wheels.*
- ○ *The station wagon had a fiberglass molded roof fairing which was beautifully finished.*

fan /fæn/ (fans)

VEHICLE COMPONENTS: ENGINE, TRANSMISSION, AND EXHAUST

NOUN A **fan** is a piece of electrical or mechanical equipment with blades that rotate. It is used to keep a machine cool or get rid of unpleasant smells.

- ○ *Despite its large capacity and a five-bladed fan, the engine tends to overheat.*
- ○ *The car has a defect in the main fan which cools the engine.*

fan belt /fæn bɛlt/ (fan belts)

VEHICLE COMPONENTS: ENGINE, TRANSMISSION, AND EXHAUST

NOUN In a vehicle engine, the **fan belt** is the belt that drives the fan which keeps the engine cool.

- ○ *The fan belt on the engine was beginning to tear.*
- ○ *The water pump stopped rotating due to a broken fan belt.*

fas|cia /feɪʃə/ (fascias)

VEHICLE COMPONENTS: BODYWORK, CONTROLS, AND ACCESSORIES

NOUN In a vehicle, **the fascia** is the part surrounding the instruments and dials.

○ *The engine instruments are set into the teak fascia.*

○ *There are five gauges on the wood-trimmed fascia.*

F

feed pump /fiːd pʌmp/ (feed pumps)

VEHICLE COMPONENTS: ENGINE, TRANSMISSION, AND EXHAUST

NOUN A **feed pump** is a pump that moves a fluid such as a fuel at a controlled rate.

○ *A low-pressure feed pump ensures that the injection pump receives a continuous flow of filtered fuel.*

○ *The fuel feed pump operates only when the engine is running.*

fend|er (In BRIT use **wing**) /fɛndər/ (fenders)

VEHICLE COMPONENTS: ENGINE, TRANSMISSION, AND EXHAUST

NOUN The **fenders** of a car are the parts of the body over the wheels.

○ *There was a fresh dent in the rear fender.*

○ *The front fenders curve over 18-inch wheels and white-lettered tires.*

▶ **COLLOCATIONS:**
front fender
rear fender

fil|ter /fɪltər/ (filters)

VEHICLE COMPONENTS: ENGINE, TRANSMISSION, AND EXHAUST

NOUN A **filter** is a device through which air, fuel, or oil is passed to remove unwanted particles.

○ *You need to clean the oil filter and completely change the oil.*

○ *Your car's air filter is extremely important in helping your engine to breathe.*

▶ COLLOCATIONS:
air filter
fuel filter
oil filter

---

fi|nal drive /faɪnᵊl dr_aɪv/ (**final drives**)

VEHICLE COMPONENTS: ENGINE, TRANSMISSION, AND EXHAUST

NOUN The **final drive** is an assembly of gears in the back axle of rear-wheel drive (= with engine power going to the rear wheels) vehicles and in the front axle of front-wheel drive (= with engine power going to the front wheels) vehicles.

○ The last set of gears in the drive train is the final drive.

○ When the final drive comes on the axle, the rotating wheels have to move at different speeds when the car negotiates a curve.

---

fire|wall /faɪərwɔl/ (**firewalls**)

VEHICLE COMPONENTS: BODYWORK, CONTROLS, AND ACCESSORIES

NOUN A **firewall** is a panel between the engine compartment and the passenger compartment in a vehicle that is intended to prevent the spread of fire from the engine.

○ The fumes probably entered his car's cockpit through the firewall, which separates the cockpit from the engine.

○ In case of a fire, the firewall protects the passengers in the car by not permitting an engine fire to enter the passenger cabin.

---

fir|ing stroke /faɪərɪŋ strovk/ (**firing strokes**)

VEHICLE COMPONENTS: ENGINE, TRANSMISSION, AND EXHAUST

NOUN The **firing stroke** is the stroke of an engine in which the fuel is burned and energy sent to the piston.

○ It is the expansion of the ignited mixture that pushes down the piston on the firing stroke.

○ The flywheel is fitted on the end of the crankshaft to store energy from the firing stroke of every cylinder.

flat bat|ter|y /flæt bætəri/ (**flat batteries**)

VEHICLE COMPONENTS: LIGHTING AND ELECTRICAL/ELECTRONIC SYSTEMS

NOUN A **flat battery** is a battery that does not have enough power to start a vehicle or provide lighting.

○ The headlamps had been left on and the car had a flat battery.

○ We had to jump-start the car because it had a flat battery.

F

flex|i|ble joint /flɛksɪbᵊl dʒɔɪnt/ (**flexible joints**)

VEHICLE COMPONENTS: ENGINE, TRANSMISSION, AND EXHAUST

NOUN A **flexible joint** is a coupling which can transmit torque between two shafts which are not aligned.

○ A flexible joint between the shafts corrects any misalignment.

○ A flexible joint allows some movement between the steering shaft and the steering box.

float /floʊt/ (**floats**)

VEHICLE COMPONENTS: BODYWORK, CONTROLS, AND ACCESSORIES

NOUN A **float** is a floating part of a fluid system, such as a carburetor or a fuel level gauge.

○ Mechanics have replaced the pin and float in the carburetor.

○ The float is at its highest when the fuel tank is full.

fly|wheel /flaɪwil/ (**flywheels**)

VEHICLE COMPONENTS: ENGINE, TRANSMISSION, AND EXHAUST

NOUN A **flywheel** is a heavy wheel that is part of some engines. It regulates the engine's rotation, making it operate at a steady speed.

○ A flywheel stores energy as it spins inside a casing.

○ A flywheel that keeps an engine turning relies on its momentum to keep going.

fold|ing top /ˈfoʊldɪŋ tɒp/ (**folding tops**)

VEHICLE COMPONENTS: BODYWORK, CONTROLS, AND ACCESSORIES

NOUN A **folding top** is a soft roof of a vehicle that can be folded down or removed.

○ *A folding top requires extra space and thus the rear seat and trunk suffer.*

○ *The convertible has a power folding top with a heated glass rear window.*

fos|sil fuel /ˈfɒsᵊl fyuəl/ (**fossil fuels**)

FUELS, OILS, EMISSIONS, AND OTHER FLUIDS

NOUN **Fossil fuel** is fuel such as coal or oil that is formed from the decayed remains of plants or animals.

○ *Burning fossil fuels uses oxygen and produces carbon dioxide.*

○ *The government thinks it would be a good idea if 10 percent of all new cars ran on hydrogen instead of fossil fuels within a decade.*

four-stroke cy|cle /ˈfɔr stroʊk saɪkᵊl/ (**four-stroke cycles**)

VEHICLE COMPONENTS: ENGINE, TRANSMISSION, AND EXHAUST

NOUN A **four-stroke cycle** is the cycle of engine operation which requires four strokes of the piston: for induction, compression, ignition, and exhaust.

○ *The leaflet explains the operation of each of the four strokes in a four-stroke cycle.*

○ *Four-stroke cycle engines allocate one up or down stroke of the piston for each of the four events.*

four-wheel drive (ABBR **4WD**) /ˈfɔr wil draɪv/ (**four-wheel drives**)

VEHICLE COMPONENTS: ENGINE, TRANSMISSION, AND EXHAUST

NOUN A **four-wheel drive** is a vehicle in which all four wheels receive power from the engine to help with steering. This makes the vehicle easier to drive on rough roads or surfaces such as sand or snow.

○ *We hired a four-wheel drive to travel across the mountainous countryside.*

○ *In a four-wheel drive, all four wheels receive torque from the engine simultaneously.*

fuel /fyuəl/ (**fuels**)

FUELS, OILS, EMISSIONS, AND OTHER FLUIDS

NOUN **Fuel** is a substance such as coal, oil, or gasoline that is burned to provide heat or power.

○ *Gasoline, LPG, hydrogen and other forms of fuel.*

○ *We all have a good idea how far our car will run on a full tank of fuel.*

TYPES OF FUEL INCLUDE:

bio-diesel, cetane, fossil fuels, gasoline, LPG

---

fuel cell /fyuəl sɛl/ (**fuel cells**)

VEHICLE COMPONENTS: LIGHTING AND ELECTRICAL/ELECTRONIC SYSTEMS

NOUN A **fuel cell** is a device, similar to a battery, that converts chemicals into electricity.

○ *Hydrogen is converted in the fuel cell into electricity.*

○ *It takes only a few seconds to start a modern gasoline-driven car, but, in cold weather, a fuel cell needs several minutes of warming up before it can produce enough power to drive off.*

---

fuel con|sump|tion /fyuəl kənsʌmpʃᵊn/

DESIGN AND PERFORMANCE

NOUN **Fuel consumption** is the rate at which an engine uses fuel, expressed in units such as miles per gallon or liters per kilometer.

○ *Engine designers strive for more power, lower fuel consumption, lighter weight, and better reliability.*

○ *Short journeys can double fuel consumption, especially when the engine is cold.*

TALKING ABOUT FUEL CONSUMPTION

To talk about using less fuel, you can say that you **cut**, **decrease**, **lower** or **reduce** fuel consumption.

To talk about using more fuel, you can say that you **increase** fuel consumption. If you use twice as much, you **double** it.

If you check how much fuel you are using, you **monitor** your fuel consumption.

---

fuel gauge or fuel gage /fyu̯əl geɪdʒ/ (**fuel gauges**)

VEHICLE COMPONENTS: BODYWORK, CONTROLS, AND ACCESSORIES

NOUN A **fuel gauge** is an instrument that shows how much fuel there is in a fuel tank.

○ *He checked the fuel gauge and saw that the tank was three-quarters full.*

○ *She was watching her falling fuel gauge, which was almost on the empty mark.*

---

fuel in|jec|tion /fyu̯əl ɪndʒɛkʃ³n/

VEHICLE COMPONENTS: ENGINE, TRANSMISSION, AND EXHAUST

NOUN **Fuel injection** is a system in the engines of some vehicles which forces fuel directly into the part of the engine where it is burned.

○ *More precise fuel injection would make engines cleaner and more economical.*

○ *Conventional fuel injection in a diesel engine involves a pump driven via a camshaft from the engine.*

---

fuel pump¹ /fyu̯əl pʌmp/ (**fuel pumps**)

VEHICLE COMPONENTS: LIGHTING AND ELECTRICAL/ELECTRONIC SYSTEMS

NOUN A **fuel pump** is a mechanical or electrical pump that draws fuel from a tank to provide the fuel supply for a carburetor or fuel injection system.

○ *The fuel pump is right next to the carburetor in this model so it sucks gas directly from the gas tank.*

○ *Allowing the gasoline level to fall to near empty risks damage to the fuel pump.*

fuel pump² /fyuəl pʌmp/ (**fuel pumps**)

VEHICLE COMPONENTS: ENGINE, TRANSMISSION, AND EXHAUST

NOUN A **fuel pump** is the high-pressure fuel injection pump of a diesel engine.

○ The fuel pump injects a definite quantity of fuel into individual cylinders.

○ You need a filter in the fuel line to prevent sediment being sucked into the fuel pump.

fuel rail /fyuəl reɪl/ (**fuel rails**)

VEHICLE COMPONENTS: ENGINE, TRANSMISSION, AND EXHAUST

NOUN A **fuel rail** is high pressure tubing which takes fuel to the injectors in an internal combustion engine.

○ The fuel passes from the fuel rail into the injectors in metal fuel pipes.

○ Be very careful when you pull off the fuel rail from the top of the injectors, as although it is made out of metal, it easily bends or breaks.

fuel sys|tem /fyuəl sɪstəm/ (**fuel systems**)

VEHICLE COMPONENTS: ENGINE, TRANSMISSION, AND EXHAUST

NOUN The **fuel system** in a vehicle is the combination of parts needed to carry fuel into and out of the engine.

○ Once a fuel system is clean the tank should be completely filled.

○ The main parts of a fuel system are the fuel tank, fuel lines, fuel pump, fuel filters, and a distribution device.

fuel tank /fyuəl tæŋk/ (**fuel tanks**)

VEHICLE COMPONENTS: ENGINE, TRANSMISSION, AND EXHAUST

NOUN The **fuel tank** is the container from which an engine draws its fuel.

○ He unscrewed the cap on the fuel tank and gasoline spilled out onto the ground.

○ I always refill my car with gasoline when the fuel tank is half empty.

fuse or **fuze** /fyuz/ (**fuses**)

VEHICLE COMPONENTS: LIGHTING AND ELECTRICAL/ELECTRONIC SYSTEMS

NOUN A **fuse** is a safety device in an electric circuit. It contains a piece of wire which melts when there is a fault, so that the flow of electricity stops.

○ *The fuse blew as she pressed the button to start the motor.*

○ *Most of the electrical subsystems on the car are protected by their own fuse.*

▶ **COLLOCATION:**
blow a fuse

Gg

gas|ket /gæskɪt/ (gaskets)

NOUN A **gasket** is a flat piece of soft material that you put between two joined surfaces in a pipe or engine in order to make sure that gas and oil cannot escape.

○ *Lubrication oil was spraying from a leaking gasket.*

○ *His car blew a gasket just a few laps into the race.*

gas|o|line (ABBR **gas**) /gæsəlin/

NOUN **Gasoline** is the fuel which is used to drive motor vehicles.

○ *Gasoline is drawn off from the gas tank by a fuel pump.*

○ *The spark plugs produce sparks that cause the gasoline to burn.*

gas tank /gæs tæŋk/ (gas tanks)

NOUN The **gas tank** in a vehicle is the container for gasoline.

○ *Gasoline is drawn off from the gas tank by a fuel pump.*

○ *A leaky gas tank leaves a strong fuel odor around the back wheels.*

gear|box /gɪərbɒks/ (gearboxes)

NOUN A **gearbox** is the system of gears in an engine or a vehicle.

○ *The car also had wider drum brakes and a five-speed gearbox.*

○ *The gear ratios of a manual gearbox can be optimized to improve the fuel economy of a passenger car.*

▶ **COLLOCATIONS:**
 five-speed gearbox
 six-speed gearbox
 manual gearbox

GEARBOX PARTS INCLUDE:

 balk ring, counter shaft, drive shaft, layshaft

---

gear ra|ti|o /gɪər reɪʃoʊ/ (**gear ratios**)

VEHICLE COMPONENTS: ENGINE, TRANSMISSION, AND EXHAUST

NOUN The **gear ratio** is the ratio of the number of turns the output shaft makes when the input shaft turns once.

○ *A gearset with a 1-inch drive gear and a 2-inch driven gear has a gear ratio of 2:1.*

○ *If the car is shifted into a higher gear, the gear ratio is reduced.*

---

gear train /gɪər treɪn/ (**gear trains**)

VEHICLE COMPONENTS: ENGINE, TRANSMISSION, AND EXHAUST

NOUN A **gear train** is a series of gears designed to achieve a particular overall gear ratio.

○ *A simple gear train has only one gear fixed to each shaft.*

○ *A gear train consists of a combination of two or more gears, mounted on rotating shafts, to transmit torque or power.*

---

glow plug /gloʊ plʌg/ (**glow plugs**)

VEHICLE COMPONENTS: ENGINE, TRANSMISSION, AND EXHAUST

NOUN A **glow plug** is an electrically heated plug that is fitted to the cylinder head of a diesel engine to make it easier to start the engine in cold conditions.

○ *The miniature motor doesn't need an ignition system, just a glow plug to get it started.*

○ *The glow plug circuit is used on the diesel engine to initially start the engine.*

▶ **SYNONYM:**
heater plug

---

gov|er|nor /gʌvərnər/ (governors)

VEHICLE COMPONENTS: ENGINE, TRANSMISSION, AND EXHAUST

NOUN A **governor** is a device which limits the maximum speed of an engine, especially a diesel engine.

○ *A lot of pickup trucks have a governor on the speed limit.*

○ *An idling speed governor is often fitted to ensure that the idling rpm does not vary with changing engine loads.*

▶ **COLLOCATION:**
speed governor

---

grease /griːs/

FUELS, OILS, EMISSIONS, AND OTHER FLUIDS

NOUN **Grease** is a thick, oily substance which is put on the moving parts of vehicles in order to make them work smoothly.

○ *The amount of dust and grease on the engine indicated it had not been touched recently.*

○ *Grease is an oil to which a thickening base has been added so that the end product is semi-solid.*

---

gut|ter|ing /gʌtərɪŋ/

VEHICLE COMPONENTS: BODYWORK, CONTROLS, AND ACCESSORIES

NOUN **Guttering** is the curved edge at the side of the roof panel of a vehicle, along which rain water is channeled away.

○ *External guttering had been replaced by rubber drainage channels inside the tops of doors.*

○ *Drip rails extend from the roof guttering of the car.*

half-shaft /hæf ʃæft/ (half-shafts)

VEHICLE COMPONENTS: ENGINE, TRANSMISSION, AND EXHAUST

NOUN The **half-shaft** or **half axle** is the shaft in a vehicle along which power is sent from the final drive to one driven wheel or a pair of wheels.

○ They needed to replace the car's offside half-shaft and there were no spares available.

○ On each half-shaft there is a bevel gear that meshes with two small bevel pinions on the inside of the crown wheel, one at the top and one at the bottom.

hand|brake /hændbreɪk/ (handbrakes)

VEHICLE COMPONENTS: BODYWORK, CONTROLS, AND ACCESSORIES

NOUN The **handbrake** in a vehicle is a brake which the driver operates with his or her hand, for example, when parking.

○ She released the handbrake, turned the ignition key, and reversed into the road.

○ The handbrake secures the car when it is parked or stationary for more than a short pause.

▶ **SYNONYMS:**
emergency brake
parking brake

▶ **COLLOCATIONS:**
apply the handbrake
release the handbrake

han|dling /ˈhændlɪŋ/

DESIGN AND PERFORMANCE

NOUN The **handling** of a vehicle is how well it responds to being driven and how easy it is to control.

○ *The integrated chassis design provides a perfect blend of light controls and positive, stable handling.*

○ *The car has smooth, sharp handling and very keen throttle response.*

hard top /ˈhɑrd tɒp/ (hard tops)

VEHICLE COMPONENTS: BODYWORK, CONTROLS, AND ACCESSORIES

NOUN A **hard top** is a vehicle that has a permanent rigid roof.

○ *This vehicle offers the combined benefits of a hard top and a convertible – better security, more protection from inclement weather and wind-in-your-hair driving when you want it.*

○ *She drives a convertible in the summer and a hard top in the winter.*

hatch|back /ˈhætʃbæk/ (hatchbacks)

VEHICLE TYPES

NOUN A **hatchback** is a car with an extra door at the back which opens upward.

○ *He drives a little three-door hatchback.*

○ *A hatchback is called a liftback when the opening area is very sloped and is lifted up to open.*

haz|ard warn|ing lamps /ˈhæzərd wɔrnɪŋ læmps/

VEHICLE COMPONENTS: LIGHTING AND ELECTRICAL/ELECTRONIC SYSTEMS

NOUN **Hazard warning lamps** are flashing lamps on each corner of a vehicle that are used to show the position of the vehicle if there has been a breakdown or an accident.

○ *Another great feature is the automatic hazard warning lamp system which operates as soon as the driver applies heavy braking or does an emergency stop.*

○ *Any attempted entry to the vehicle will cause the siren to sound and the hazard warning lamps to flash for 30 seconds.*

head|er tank /ˈhɛdər tæŋk/ (**header tanks**)

VEHICLE COMPONENTS: BODYWORK, CONTROLS, AND ACCESSORIES

NOUN A **header tank** is a container of liquid positioned at a higher level than a main tank, so that the level of pressure can be maintained.

○ *The coolant in the radiator header tank should have a mix of water and antifreeze.*

○ *Any loss of coolant will show up first at the header tank, and level sensors are available to detect this.*

head|lamp /ˈhɛdlæmp/ (**headlamps**)

VEHICLE COMPONENTS: LIGHTING AND ELECTRICAL/ELECTRONIC SYSTEMS

NOUN A **headlamp** is a lamp on the front of a vehicle which provides light ahead of it.

○ *He tried to shield his eyes from the glare of the truck's headlamp.*

○ *Driving with only one headlamp is dangerous, not so much for the driver's visibility as for the visibility of the car to other drivers.*

▶ **SYNONYM:**
   headlight

> **TYPES OF LAMPS AND LIGHTS INCLUDE:**
>
> backup lamp, courtesy light, hazard warning lamp, headlamp, turn signal

head|li|ning /ˈhɛdlaɪnɪŋ/

VEHICLE COMPONENTS: BODYWORK, CONTROLS, AND ACCESSORIES

NOUN **Headlining** is the fabric roof lining or ceiling of the body of a vehicle.

○ *Changes made inside the car include a lighter colored headlining and some extra chrome touches.*

○ *The standard headlining was in gray felt and the rear package shelf was also covered in a felt material.*

head|rest /hɛdrɛst/ (headrests)

VEHICLE COMPONENTS: BODYWORK, CONTROLS, AND ACCESSORIES

NOUN A **headrest** is the part of the back of a seat in a vehicle on which you can lean your head, especially one on the front seat.

○ The headrest at the back of a driver's seat should help to prevent whiplash injuries.

○ The federal government will require auto makers to install in minivans, pickup trucks, and multi-purpose vehicles the same front-seat headrests long required on passenger cars.

head re|straint /hɛd rɪstreɪnt/ (head restraints)

VEHICLE COMPONENTS: BODYWORK, CONTROLS, AND ACCESSORIES

NOUN A **head restraint** is a headrest or pad firmly supported behind the head of a driver or passenger to minimize whiplash injury in a crash.

○ The injury was caused by her head being thrown back against the head restraint during the collision.

○ The head restraint should be at a height which positions its center directly in line with the back of the driver's head.

head-up dis|play /hɛd ʌp dɪspleɪ/ (head-up displays)

VEHICLE COMPONENTS: BODYWORK, CONTROLS, AND ACCESSORIES

NOUN The **head-up display** is an instrument display reflected in the windshield of a vehicle that allows the driver to see essential instruments without having to look down at the instrument panel.

○ This model has an optional head-up display that projects key driver information onto the windshield.

○ The camera scans the road ahead for heat signatures of the human body, and its images are projected on to a head-up display on the windshield.

heav|y goods ve|hi|cle (ABBR HGV) /hɛvi gʊdz viːkəl/ (heavy goods vehicles)

VEHICLE TYPES

NOUN A **heavy goods vehicle** is a large vehicle intended for the transportation of heavy loads. Drivers of these vehicles must have a special training and license.

○ *You need a special license to drive a heavy goods vehicle.*

○ *A heavy goods vehicle is a goods vehicle which exceeds 7.5 tonnes permissible maximum weight.*

---

hood /hʊd/ (**hoods**)

VEHICLE COMPONENTS: BODYWORK, CONTROLS, AND ACCESSORIES

NOUN The **hood** of a vehicle is the metal cover over the engine at the front.

○ *Anti-theft features include a device that shuts down the gas and ignition, and seals the hood shut.*

○ *Smoke was pouring from under the hood of the car.*

▶ **COLLOCATIONS:**
   open the hood
   shut the hood

---

hor|i|zon|tal|ly op|posed /hɔrɪzɒntᵊli əpoʊzd/

VEHICLE COMPONENTS: ENGINE, TRANSMISSION, AND EXHAUST

ADJECTIVE A **horizontally opposed** engine has the cylinders set horizontally at either side of the crankshaft.

○ *The horizontally opposed 4 cylinder was a very popular engine installed in the Volkswagen Beetle.*

○ *The horizontally opposed engine produces regular pulses but they appear on alternate sides of the engine.*

---

horn /hɔrn/ (**horns**)

VEHICLE COMPONENTS: BODYWORK, CONTROLS, AND ACCESSORIES

NOUN On a vehicle such as a car, the **horn** is the device that makes a loud noise as a signal or warning.

○ *He sounded the car horn.*

○ *Proper use of a car horn as a warning can avoid serious accidents.*

▶ **COLLOCATION:**
   sound the horn

horse|pow|er /hɔːrspaʊər/

NOUN **Horsepower** is a unit of power used for measuring how powerful an engine is.

○ This vehicle has a 300-horsepower engine.

○ The term horsepower describes how much power an engine can produce, and is directly related to how much speed a car can achieve.

hub /hʌb/ (hubs)

NOUN The **hub** of a wheel is the part at the center containing the wheel bearings.

○ These protective shields fit in between the wheel and the hub to keep the wheels free of dirt and brake dust.

○ The wheel bearings had failed, and the entire wheel hub had come off the truck's axle.

hub|cap /hʌbkæp/ (hubcaps)

NOUN A **hubcap** is a metal or plastic disk that covers and protects the center of a wheel on a vehicle.

○ The hubcaps were missing from nearside wheels.

○ He got a tire iron out of the trunk and took the hubcaps off the wheels of his car.

hy|brid ve|hi|cle (ABBR **hybrid**) /haɪbrɪd viːɪkᵊl/ (**hybrid vehicles**)

NOUN A **hybrid vehicle** is a vehicle using two different forms of power, such as an electric motor and an internal combustion engine, or an electric motor with a battery and fuel cells for energy storage.

○ Sales of the gas-electric hybrid vehicle reached record-breaking levels in May.

○ The hybrid vehicle does save on fuel and reduces pollution, depending on the degree of hybridization.

hy|drau|lic brake /haɪdrɔlɪk breɪk/ (**hydraulic brakes**)

VEHICLE COMPONENTS: BRAKES, STEERING, WHEELS, TIRES, AND SUSPENSION

NOUN A **hydraulic brake** is a brake activated by hydraulic pressure.

○ *The chassis, suspension, and new hydraulic brake system help make this one of the easiest and safest cars on the road to drive.*

○ *Brake fluid is the liquid used in the hydraulic brake system to stop or slow the car.*

hy|dro|car|bon /haɪdroʊkɑrbən/ (**hydrocarbons**)

FUELS, OILS, EMISSIONS, AND OTHER FLUIDS

NOUN A **hydrocarbon** is a chemical compound that is a mixture of hydrogen and carbon. It is the main constituent of liquid and gaseous fuels.

○ *These vehicles, powered by fuel cells, will be able to run on hydrogen extracted from conventional hydrocarbon fuel.*

○ *There are hundreds of partially burnt hydrocarbons present in the diesel exhaust.*

hy|dro|plan|ing (In BRIT use **aquaplaning**) /haɪdroʊpleɪnɪŋ/

DESIGN AND PERFORMANCE

NOUN **Hydroplaning** is a situation in which a vehicle tire rides up on a thin surface of water, losing contact with the pavement, and resulting in sudden loss of control.

○ *Some experts believe that hydroplaning accounts for the majority of single-car accidents in wet weather.*

○ *Hydroplaning can happen when a cushion of water is built up in front of fast-moving tires.*

i|dle speed /aɪdᵊl spid/

VEHICLE COMPONENTS: ENGINE, TRANSMISSION, AND EXHAUST

NOUN The **idle speed** of an engine is its speed when it has no load and is on a minimum throttle setting.

○ *The idle speed is high when the truck is cold.*

○ *When you stop at the traffic lights, or when you disengage the clutch to change the gears, the engine works in idle speed.*

ig|ni|tion¹ /ɪgnɪʃᵊn/

VEHICLE COMPONENTS: LIGHTING AND ELECTRICAL/ELECTRONIC SYSTEMS

NOUN **Ignition** is the process of making the fuel start to burn in an engine so that a vehicle can start to move.

○ *A massive explosion accompanies the ignition of refined gasoline or fuel oil.*

○ *Ignition of the compressed fuel mixture takes place when the spark flame reaches it.*

ig|ni|tion² /ɪgnɪʃᵊn/

VEHICLE COMPONENTS: LIGHTING AND ELECTRICAL/ELECTRONIC SYSTEMS

NOUN In a car engine, the **ignition** is the part where the fuel is ignited.

○ *The device automatically disconnects the ignition.*

○ *She pulled over to the side of the road, and switched off the ignition.*

ig|ni|tion³ /ɪɡnɪʃ°n/

VEHICLE COMPONENTS: LIGHTING AND ELECTRICAL/ELECTRONIC SYSTEMS

NOUN Inside a car, **the ignition** is the part where you turn the key so that the engine starts.

○ *Abruptly he turned the ignition key and started the engine.*

○ *You should never leave the keys of your car in the ignition.*

ig|ni|tion coil /ɪɡnɪʃ°n kɔɪl/ (**ignition coils**)

VEHICLE COMPONENTS: ENGINE, TRANSMISSION, AND EXHAUST

NOUN The **ignition coil** is the part that provides the high tension voltage for the spark in spark ignition engines.

○ *The misfire could be caused by poor insulation of the ignition wires or a faulty ignition coil.*

○ *The ignition coil is used to produce the high voltage for the sparks.*

ig|ni|tion tim|ing /ɪɡnɪʃ°n taɪmɪŋ/

VEHICLE COMPONENTS: ENGINE, TRANSMISSION, AND EXHAUST

NOUN **Ignition timing** is the timing of the spark relative to the piston top dead center in a spark ignition engine.

○ *You can adjust the ignition timing to suit a fuel of a lower octane rating.*

○ *The ignition timing ensures that the spark plug ignites the fuel at the optimum moment.*

im|mo|bi|liz|er /ɪmoʊbɪlaɪzər/ (**immobilizers**)

VEHICLE COMPONENTS: LIGHTING AND ELECTRICAL/ELECTRONIC SYSTEMS

NOUN An **immobilizer** is a device on a vehicle that prevents it from starting unless a special key is used, so that no one can steal the car.

○ *The car has a standard anti-theft ignition immobilizer.*

○ *A spokesman for the Insurance Institute for Highway Safety said immobilizers have been the most effective way to stop thefts.*

im|pact /ˈɪmpækt/ (**impacts**)

NOUN An **impact** is the action of a vehicle hitting another vehicle or object, or the force with which one hits the other.

○ *The force of the impact burst both tires and plucked off a wheel.*

○ *Motor industry research is focused on making impacts between cars and SUVs safer.*

▶ **COLLOCATION:**
suffer an impact

in|board brakes /ˈɪnbɔrd breɪks/

VEHICLE COMPONENTS: BRAKES, STEERING, WHEELS, TIRES, AND SUSPENSION

NOUN **Inboard brakes** are brakes located close to the center of the vehicle rather than at the wheel hub.

○ *Inboard brakes are less easy to keep cool than outboard ones.*

○ *For the auto maker, inboard brakes represent a cost saving, as calipers can be built right into the differential case instead of being made separately.*

in-car en|ter|tain|ment /ɪn kar ɛntərteɪnmənt/

VEHICLE COMPONENTS: LIGHTING AND ELECTRICAL/ELECTRONIC SYSTEMS

NOUN **In-car entertainment** is a sound system consisting of, for example, a radio or compact disc player, that is designed for easy operation by the driver, and to be unaffected by vibration. In larger vehicles, this system can include television and DVD player.

○ *The in-car entertainment market is growing as the technology such as DVD and home theater equipment has been adapted for the road.*

○ *The basic car radio was the standard in-car entertainment for many years, until the digital era took hold.*

in|de|pend|ent sus|pen|sion /ɪndɪpɛndənt səspɛnʃᵊn/

VEHICLE COMPONENTS: BRAKES, STEERING, WHEELS, TIRES, AND SUSPENSION

NOUN **Independent suspension** is a suspension system in which the movement of one wheel is not directly transferred to the other.

○ *The car comes in either manual or automatic transmission with comfort guaranteed by fully independent suspension.*

○ *Handling was satisfying, with the four wheel independent suspension providing a near-ideal combination of passenger comfort and handling stiffness.*

---

in|di|ca|tor /ɪndɪkeɪtər/ (**indicators**)

DESIGN AND PERFORMANCE

NOUN An **indicator** is an instrument that shows engine cylinder pressure during a working cycle.

○ *Adjust the connections until the cylinder pressure indicator reading does not fall within 1 minute after closing the cylinder valve.*

○ *The indicator keeps the graphical record of pressure inside the cylinder during the piston stroke.*

> **US/UK ENGLISH**
>
> In British English, indicators are the flashing lights that tell you that a vehicle is going to turn left or right. In American English, these are called **turn signals**.

---

in|di|ca|tor di|a|gram /ɪndɪkeɪtər daɪəgræm/ (**indicator diagrams**)

DESIGN AND PERFORMANCE

NOUN An **indicator diagram** is a map of cylinder pressure plotted against stroke or degrees of rotation for the power stroke or complete cycle of an engine.

○ *The fuel/air ratio of the charge influences the rate of combustion and has an effect on indicator diagrams.*

○ *If you measure the area under the indicator diagram, you can find out the power the engine is producing.*

in|di|rect in|jec|tion (ABBR **ID**) /ˌɪndaɪrɛkt ɪndʒɛkʃ°n/

VEHICLE COMPONENTS: ENGINE, TRANSMISSION, AND EXHAUST

NOUN **Indirect injection** is a diesel engine injection system in which ignition is started before the burning mixture enters the main combustion chamber.

○ *Indirect injection engines are cheaper to build and it is easier to produce smooth, quiet-running vehicles.*

○ *In indirect injection engines, the fuel and air are premixed in a prechamber before passing into the rest of the chamber.*

in|duc|tion /ɪndʌkʃ°n/

VEHICLE COMPONENTS: ENGINE, TRANSMISSION, AND EXHAUST

NOUN **Induction** is the drawing in of air or an air/fuel mixture into an engine.

○ *Can detergents help keep the induction and fuelling systems of an engine free of deposits?*

○ *The device measures the velocity of air flowing into the engine's induction system and the temperature of that air.*

in|duc|tion stroke /ɪndʌkʃ°n stroʊk/ (**induction strokes**)

VEHICLE COMPONENTS: ENGINE, TRANSMISSION, AND EXHAUST

NOUN The **induction stroke** is the stroke of the piston in an internal combustion engine in which working fluid is drawn into the cylinder.

○ *Most of the liquid fuel entering the cylinder is probably vaporized during the induction stroke.*

○ *The fuel-air mixture is introduced into each cylinder during its induction stroke.*

▶ SYNONYMS:
  intake stroke
  suction stroke

in|jec|tion pump /ɪndʒɛkʃᵊn pʌmp/ (**injection pumps**)

VEHICLE COMPONENTS: ENGINE, TRANSMISSION, AND EXHAUST

NOUN An **injection pump** is a device that supplies fuel under pressure to the injector of a fuel injection system.

○ *The engine was rebuilt but the fuel injection pump did not work well.*

○ *The basic diesel injection system consists of injection pump, injection lines, injectors, and glow plugs.*

in|jec|tor /ɪndʒɛktər/ (**injectors**)

VEHICLE COMPONENTS: ENGINE, TRANSMISSION, AND EXHAUST

NOUN An **injector** is a device for introducing fuel under pressure into the combustion system of an engine.

○ *The vibration of the four-cylinder engine cracked a fuel injector pipe.*

○ *Larger injectors increased fuel flow to the 2.4-liter turbocharged engine.*

in|jec|tor noz|zle /ɪndʒɛktər nɒzᵊl/ (**injector nozzles**)

VEHICLE COMPONENTS: ENGINE, TRANSMISSION, AND EXHAUST

NOUN An **injector nozzle** is a fine sprayer through which fuel is injected into an engine.

○ *The top of the injector nozzle has a lot of holes to deliver a spray of diesel fuel into the cylinder.*

○ *The higher the pressure, the smaller the injector nozzle openings can be, producing smaller pulses that provide better fuel atomization.*

in|ner tube /ɪnər tub/ (**inner tubes**)

VEHICLE COMPONENTS: BRAKES, STEERING, WHEELS, TIRES, AND SUSPENSION

NOUN An **inner tube** is a rubber tube containing air that is inside a car tire.

○ *They are manufactured from the strong black rubber from the inner tube of a car tire.*

○ *She removed the flattened tire from its wheel, and pulled out the inner tube to find its leaking hole.*

in|stru|ment pan|el /ˌɪnstrəmənt pænᵊl/ (**instrument panels**)

VEHICLE COMPONENTS: BODYWORK, CONTROLS, AND ACCESSORIES

NOUN The **instrument panel** of a vehicle is the panel where the dials and switches are located.

○ *The trip computer readout is mounted on the instrument panel of the car.*

○ *The instrument panel is a cluster of gauges and switches that is mounted on the driver's side of the dashboard.*

---

in|take man|i|fold /ˌɪnteɪk mænɪfoʊld/ (**intake manifolds**)

VEHICLE COMPONENTS: ENGINE, TRANSMISSION, AND EXHAUST

NOUN An **intake manifold** or **induction manifold** is a manifold which distributes working fluid to different parts of a vehicle's engine.

○ *A new larger exhaust system and revised twin-chamber intake manifold boost power in this model.*

○ *Separate pipes take the gasoline to jets attached to the intake manifold. Usually there is one jet per cylinder.*

---

in|take valve /ˌɪnteɪk vælv/ (**intake valves**)

VEHICLE COMPONENTS: ENGINE, TRANSMISSION, AND EXHAUST

NOUN An **intake valve** is a valve that controls the amount of working fluid entering the cylinder of an engine.

○ *The variable valve timing meant that one intake valve was opened fully while the second was opened only slightly.*

○ *When the intake valve for a particular cylinder is open, the air flows through the throttle body, which is mounted on the intake manifold.*

---

in|ter|cool|er /ˌɪntərkulər/ (**intercoolers**)

VEHICLE COMPONENTS: ENGINE, TRANSMISSION, AND EXHAUST

NOUN An **intercooler** is a device that removes heat from pressure-charged air.

○ *The air-water intercooler is said to be four times as effective as the more usual air-air type.*

○ *The front dashboard has a larger, lower grille to feed more air to the turbo intercooler.*

▶ **SYNONYM:**
aftercooler

---

in|ter|nal com|bus|tion en|gine (ABBR **ICE**) /ɪntɜrnəl

kəmbʌstʃən ɛndʒɪn/ (**internal combustion engines**)

VEHICLE COMPONENTS: ENGINE, TRANSMISSION, AND EXHAUST

NOUN An **internal combustion engine** is an engine that creates its energy by burning fuel inside itself. Most cars have internal combustion engines.

○ *A typical internal combustion engine harnesses only a quarter of the specific energy of gasoline.*

○ *We can reduce oil dependence by using alternatives to the gasoline-powered internal combustion engine, such as fuel-cell systems, which can derive hydrogen from natural gas.*

Jj

jack /dʒæk/ (jacks)

VEHICLE COMPONENTS: BODYWORK, CONTROLS, AND ACCESSORIES

NOUN A **jack** is a device for lifting a vehicle off the ground.

○ *There was a truck there with a jack under the back wheel.*

○ *The car has built-in hydraulic jacks, which facilitate rapid tire changes.*

---

jack|knife /dʒæknaɪf/ (jackknifes, jackknifed, jackknifing)

DESIGN AND PERFORMANCE

VERB If a truck that is in two parts **jackknifes**, the back part swings around at a sharp angle to the front part in an uncontrolled way as the truck is moving.

○ *A truck pulling a camper jackknifed and brought traffic to a standstill.*

○ *The tractor-trailer jackknifed across both lanes of the icy highway.*

RELATED WORDS

The following words describe other problematic things that a vehicle may do:

backfire
produce an explosion in the exhaust pipe

skid
slide sideways or forward

stall
the engine suddenly stops

jet /dʒɛt/ (**jets**)

VEHICLE COMPONENTS: ENGINE, TRANSMISSION, AND EXHAUST

NOUN A **jet** is a hole through which liquid can pass at a controlled rate, as in a carburetor.

○ *You can enrich the output from the carburetor jet.*

○ *Air and fuel are mixed in the carburetor and sent out through a jet as a high-pressure spray.*

jump lead /dʒʌmp liːd/ (**jump leads**)

VEHICLE COMPONENTS: LIGHTING AND ELECTRICAL/ELECTRONIC SYSTEMS

NOUN **Jump leads** are thick electrical leads that are used to connect a flat battery in a vehicle to an external charged battery, such as the battery of another vehicle, so that the first vehicle can be started.

○ *Connect the red jump lead between the positive terminal posts of both batteries.*

○ *Jump leads help start an engine when the battery is low or flat.*

Kk

---

king|pin /ˈkɪŋpɪn/ (kingpins)

VEHICLE COMPONENTS: BRAKES, STEERING, WHEELS, TIRES, AND SUSPENSION

NOUN The **kingpin** is the shaft about which a steered wheel pivots.

- ○ Place the top of the gauge in contact with the apron plate and slide over the kingpin.

- ○ The wheel, hub, and steering knuckle all pivot around the kingpin.

---

knock /nɒk/

VEHICLE COMPONENTS: ENGINE, TRANSMISSION, AND EXHAUST

NOUN **Knock** is the noise caused by part of the air-fuel mixture in an engine cylinder burning before the normal combustion started by a spark.

- ○ Knock has less to do with the mechanical operation of an engine than with the fuel that engine uses.

- ○ Lead was added to gasoline to stop engine knock in automobiles.

lam|i|nat|ed glass /ˈlæmɪneɪtɪd glæs/

VEHICLE COMPONENTS: BODYWORK, CONTROLS, AND ACCESSORIES

NOUN **Laminated glass** is safety glass in which a transparent plastic film is placed between plates of glass.

○ *Long used in car windshields, laminated glass is now widely used in architecture.*

○ *The car has laminated glass side windows for improved security and noise insulation.*

lamp /læmp/ (**lamps**)

VEHICLE COMPONENTS: BODYWORK, CONTROLS, AND ACCESSORIES

NOUN A **lamp** is a lighting unit in a vehicle.

○ *In the event of a damper fault, the dashboard warning lamp lights up to warn the driver.*

○ *The government should legislate against the use of fog lamps in fine weather, as they impair the vision of oncoming drivers.*

lap and di|ag|o|nal belt /læp ənd daɪˈægənəl bɛlt/ (**lap and diagonal belts**)

VEHICLE COMPONENTS: BODYWORK, CONTROLS, AND ACCESSORIES

NOUN A **lap and diagonal belt** is a strap attached to a seat in a vehicle that extends horizontally in front of the hips and diagonally from the outer shoulder across the chest. You fasten it across your body in order to prevent yourself being thrown out of the seat if there is a sudden movement or stop.

○ *A booster seat enables a child, from 4 years old, to use an adult lap and diagonal belt.*

○ *The provision of a lap and diagonal belt for the center rear seat is a good safety feature of this model.*

▶ **SYNONYMS:**
lap and shoulder belt
three-point belt

---

lay|shaft /leɪʃæft/ (**layshafts**)

VEHICLE COMPONENTS: ENGINE, TRANSMISSION, AND EXHAUST

NOUN The **layshaft** is the shaft in a gearbox that runs parallel to the main shaft and carries the paired gear wheels or pinions.

○ *Failure of a layshaft had caused loss of oil to the main bearings.*

○ *The extended layshaft supports a pair of high and low speed gears.*

---

lead ac|id bat|ter|y /lɛd æsɪd bætəri/ (**lead acid batterys**)

VEHICLE COMPONENTS: LIGHTING AND ELECTRICAL/ELECTRONIC SYSTEMS

NOUN A **lead acid battery** is a 12-volt battery for passenger cars and light commercial vehicles consisting of lead-acid cells in series.

○ *The car's power comes from a 6-volt lead acid battery that, when fully charged, can run up to 80 km.*

○ *A lead acid battery uses the chemical reaction between lead and sulfuric acid to generate electricity.*

---

lead-free /lɛd friː/

FUELS, OILS, EMISSIONS, AND OTHER FLUIDS

ADJECTIVE **Lead-free** gasoline is made without lead, or has no lead added to it.

○ *Many classic cars cannot run on lead-free gasoline.*

○ *Levels of lead in the environment have plummeted in the country since the advent of lead-free gasoline.*

▶ **SYNONYM:**
unleaded

leaf spring /lif sprɪŋ/ (**leaf springs**)

VEHICLE COMPONENTS: ENGINE, TRANSMISSION, AND EXHAUST

NOUN A **leaf spring** is a spring built from narrow, flat blades which resist load in bending.

○ *Technological changes in the automotive industry have decreased the need for leaf spring suspensions.*

○ *The change from transverse leaf spring to coil spring rear suspension has undoubtedly been a great improvement.*

lean mix|ture /liːn mɪkstʃər/ (**lean mixtures**)

FUELS, OILS, EMISSIONS, AND OTHER FLUIDS

NOUN A **lean mixture** is a fuel/air mixture containing a relatively low proportion of fuel.

○ *A lean mixture can be caused by too little fuel or too much air.*

○ *Too much oxygen indicates a lean mixture and the need for less fuel.*

RELATED WORDS

Compare **lean mixture** with the following words:

rich mixture
a fuel/air mixture containing an excessive proportion of fuel.

enrichment
the process of increasing the proportion of fuel to air in a carburetor.

---

li|cense plate (In BRIT use **number plate**) /laɪsᵊns pleɪt/ (**license plates**)

VEHICLE COMPONENTS: BODYWORK, CONTROLS, AND ACCESSORIES

NOUN A **license plate** is a sign on the back, and in some places also on the front, of a vehicle that shows its license number.

○ *The license plate is mounted in a recessed housing between the tail lamps.*

○ *She noted the number on the license plate of the car, and had the registration traced.*

light /laɪt/ (**lights**)

VEHICLE COMPONENTS: BODYWORK, CONTROLS, AND ACCESSORIES

NOUN A **light** is a window in a passenger vehicle.

○ *The car is a six-light saloon in black with gray trim.*

○ *As well as referring to headlights, the word light can also mean a window or part of a window divided by a vertical support.*

live ax|le /laɪv æksᵊl/ (**live axles**)

VEHICLE COMPONENTS: BRAKES, STEERING, WHEELS, TIRES, AND SUSPENSION

NOUN A **live axle** is an axle that transmits power to a pair of wheels.

○ *The rear rig is a live axle with steel leaf springs.*

○ *The switch from live axle to front independent suspension on the latest models has improved the ride quality.*

lock¹ /lɒk/

VEHICLE COMPONENTS: BRAKES, STEERING, WHEELS, TIRES, AND SUSPENSION

NOUN **Lock** is the maximum angle to which steered wheels can be turned.

○ *Listen for a clicking noise from the front wheels when the steering is turned on full lock.*

○ *On manual steering cars, turn the steering from lock to lock at least five times to settle the steering components.*

▶ **COLLOCATION:**
lock to ~

lock² /lɒk/ (**locks**)

VEHICLE COMPONENTS: BODYWORK, CONTROLS, AND ACCESSORIES

NOUN The **lock** on a vehicle door is the device which is used to keep it shut and prevent other people from opening it. Locks are opened with a key.

○ *She approached the car and put her key in the lock.*

○ *He tried to open the car door, but the lock had jammed.*

lock³ /lɒk/

VEHICLE COMPONENTS: BRAKES, STEERING, WHEELS, TIRES, AND SUSPENSION

NOUN **Lock** is the angle of rotation of steered wheels about the steering axis.

○ *On a level field, it may be possible to rely entirely on a fixed steered-wheel lock to keep the tractor on course.*

○ *At low speeds and full lock of the wheel left or right the front end of the vehicle jumps.*

▶ **COLLOCATION:**
full lock

lock⁴ /lɒk/ (**locks, locked, locking**)

VEHICLE COMPONENTS: BODYWORK, CONTROLS, AND ACCESSORIES

VERB When you **lock** a vehicle door, you fasten it with a key so that other people cannot open it.

○ *He slammed the car door shut and locked it.*

○ *Check that all the doors on the car are locked.*

▶ **COLLOCATION:**
lock the door

low-pro|file /loʊ ˈproʊfaɪl/

VEHICLE COMPONENTS: BRAKES, STEERING, WHEELS, TIRES, AND SUSPENSION

ADJECTIVE **Low-profile** tires have a wide tread and a thin sidewall.

○ *A low-profile tire will quicken the response to steering changes.*

○ *The increased lateral stiffness of a low-profile tire will increase the sensitivity to camber variations.*

L|P|G /ɛl pi dʒi/ (short for **liquefied petroleum gas**)

FUELS, OILS, EMISSIONS, AND OTHER FLUIDS

ABBREVIATION **LPG** is an alternative type of fuel for vehicles, consisting of hydrocarbon gases in liquid form.

○ *There will be a $1000 government grant for each new LPG vehicle.*

○ *His vehicles are equipped to run on LPG in order to restrict pollution.*

Mm

Mac|Pher|son strut /məkfɜ̠rsᵊn strʌt/ (**MacPherson struts**)

NOUN A **MacPherson strut** is a form of independent front suspension. Named after US engineer Earle MacPherson.

○ *The car uses MacPherson strut suspension up front and a twist-beam independent set-up in the rear.*

○ *The MacPherson strut front and trailing arm independent rear can receive very little modification.*

man|i|fold /mænɪfoʊld/ (**manifolds**)

NOUN A **manifold** is a system of pipes that divides a flow and carries it to more than one place or that brings a flow from a number of places to a single place.

○ *The engine was given a new inlet manifold and modern carburetor.*

○ *In tests, the new manifold cut the back pressures in the exhaust system enough to boost engine power by between three and five percent.*

man|u|al steer|ing /mænyuəl stɪərɪŋ/

NOUN **Manual steering** is steering in which the driver does all the work, without the help of mechanical power.

○ *Change-over from automatic to manual steering should be possible under any conditions.*

○ *The manual steering is delightfully fluid and not so much heavy as it is low geared.*

> **RELATED WORDS**
>
> Compare **manual steering** with **power steering**, where power from the engine is used to make it easier for the driver to steer.

man|u|al trans|mis|sion /mænyuəl trænzmɪʃᵊn/ (**manual transmissions**)

VEHICLE COMPONENTS: ENGINE, TRANSMISSION, AND EXHAUST

NOUN **Manual transmission** is a type of transmission in which the gears are changed by a lever operated by the driver of a vehicle.

○ *A five-speed manual transmission is standard on both engines.*

○ *The car is available in automatic and manual transmission.*

mas|ter cyl|in|der /mæstər sɪlɪndər/ (**master cylinders**)

VEHICLE COMPONENTS: BRAKES, STEERING, WHEELS, TIRES, AND SUSPENSION

NOUN The **master cylinder** is the main source of pressure in a hydraulic system such as a brake or clutch system.

○ *I put my foot on the clutch pedal, to find that the master cylinder had seized solid.*

○ *A new brake master cylinder has also helped to improve stopping power.*

mean pis|ton speed /min pɪstᵊn spid/ (**mean piston speeds**)

VEHICLE COMPONENTS: ENGINE, TRANSMISSION, AND EXHAUST

NOUN The **mean piston speed** is the distance traveled by a piston in a specified amount of time.

○ *To make comparisons between engines of different sizes, it is common to calculate the mean piston speed.*

○ *The mean piston speed is the piston speed averaged over one engine revolution.*

mild steel /maɪld stil/

MATERIALS

NOUN **Mild steel** is a type of low-carbon steel that is widely used for vehicle bodywork and chassis construction.

○ Some new alloys have the properties of nearly the same stiffness and strength of mild steel.

○ Mild steel contains iron with small amounts of carbon, and it is used for car bodies.

min|er|al oil /mɪnərəl ɔɪl/

FUELS, OILS, EMISSIONS, AND OTHER FLUIDS

NOUN **Mineral oil** is a light hydrocarbon which is a product of petroleum and is used as a lubricant.

○ To ensure that the rollers glide easily, industrial grade mineral oil is used.

○ Brake fluid is highly corrosive and lacks the lubricating properties of a mineral oil.

mod|el /mɒdəl/ (models)

DESIGN AND PERFORMANCE

NOUN A particular **model** of a vehicle is a particular version of it.

○ The Sport model features leather trim and bucket seats.

○ This model offers exceptional space and comfort with the maneuverability of much smaller sedans.

mon|o|coque /mɒnəkɒk/ (monocoques)

VEHICLE COMPONENTS: BODYWORK, CONTROLS, AND ACCESSORIES

NOUN A **monocoque** is a structure, such as a car body, that consists of a rigid shell.

○ It is a superb little car with a glassfiber monocoque.

○ Monocoque structures are generally much lighter than frame structures, which is why most car bodies are made this way.

> **PRONUNCIATION**
>
> Note that this word has only three syllables. It comes from the
> French *coque*, which means "shell."

---

mo|tor /mo͞otər/ (motors)

VEHICLE COMPONENTS: ENGINE, TRANSMISSION, AND EXHAUST

NOUN The **motor** in a vehicle is the part that uses electricity or fuel to
produce movement, so that the vehicle can work.

○ *She got into the car and started the motor.*

○ *Electric motors can be powerful and they deliver large amounts of low-speed
pulling power.*

---

mo|tor|cy|cle /mo͞otərsaɪkəl/ (motorcycles)

VEHICLE TYPES

NOUN A **motorcycle** is a vehicle with two wheels and an engine.

○ *The package was delivered by a motorcycle dispatch rider.*

○ *Under existing laws, student drivers as young as 16 cannot ride motorcycles
with a larger engine capacity than 250cc.*

---

mo|tor scoot|er /mo͞otər sku̅tər/ (motor scooters)

VEHICLE TYPES

NOUN A **motor scooter** is a motor bicycle with small wheels.

○ *He rides a 50cc motor scooter.*

○ *The motor scooter was developed in Italy as the feminine equivalent of the
larger, more masculine motorbike.*

---

muf|fler (In BRIT use **silencer**) /mʌflər/ (mufflers)

VEHICLE COMPONENTS: ENGINE, TRANSMISSION, AND EXHAUST

NOUN A **muffler** is a device on a car exhaust that makes it quieter.

○ *Two specially-tailored stainless steel exhaust pipes run through the custom-
built mufflers.*

○ *The legislation states that if a car's modified muffler is noticeably louder than noise that would come from the original exhaust system it should be ordered off the road.*

---

mul|ti|grade oil /mʌltɪgreɪd ɔɪl/

FUELS, OILS, EMISSIONS, AND OTHER FLUIDS

NOUN **Multigrade oil** is engine or gear oil which works well at both low and high temperatures.

○ *Multigrade oil will make cold starting easier in winter.*

○ *A multigrade oil is thinner at low temperatures and thicker at high temperatures.*

M

Nn

---

nee|dle valve /ni:dəl vælv/ (needle valves)

NOUN A **needle valve** is a valve in which a pointed rod controls the rate at which a fluid flows.

○ The fuel/air mixture is generally weakened by worn needles and needle valve seats.

○ When the float drops, the needle valve reopens and allows more fuel to enter the float chamber.

---

neu|tral /nu:trəl/

NOUN **Neutral** is the position between the gears of a vehicle, in which the gears are not connected to the engine.

○ She put the car into neutral.

○ He eased the throttles back to idle and shifted them into neutral.

▶ COLLOCATION:
  in neutral

TALKING ABOUT GEARS

If a vehicle is **in neutral**, the gears are not connected to the engine. If it is **in gear**, the gears are connected.

If a vehicle is **in reverse**, it is ready to go backward.

To use a different gear, you **shift gear** or **change gear**.

When you start to drive, you should be in **first gear** or **low gear**.

When you are driving fast, you should be in **top gear**.

When you want to stop and park, the vehicle should be in **Park**.

nick|el /nɪkᵊl/

MATERIALS

NOUN **Nickel** is a silver-colored metal that is used in making steel.

○ *About 60 percent of nickel production is used to make stainless steel.*

○ *China's industrial expansion has also caused shortages of nickel and other raw materials used in steel production.*

ni|tro|gen ox|ides (ABBR **NOx**) /naɪtrədʒən ɒksaɪdz/

FUELS, OILS, EMISSIONS, AND OTHER FLUIDS

NOUN **Nitrogen oxides** are compounds of nitrogen and oxygen produced during combustion.

○ *The government has introduced a series of Clean Air Act rules related to nitrogen oxides.*

○ *Vehicles running on fuel cells produce virtually none of the pollutants associated with gasoline engines, such as nitrogen oxides and the greenhouse gas carbon dioxide.*

nor|mal|ly as|pi|rat|ed /nɔrməli æspəreɪtɪd/

VEHICLE COMPONENTS: ENGINE, TRANSMISSION, AND EXHAUST

ADJECTIVE A **normally aspirated** or **naturally aspirated** engine breathes air at atmospheric pressure.

○ *The new model can be ordered with a normally aspirated or turbocharged four-cylinder engine.*

○ *Supercharged engines can be more prone to detonation than normally aspirated engines.*

▶ COLLOCATION:
normally aspirated engine

N|V|H /ɛn vi eɪtʃ/ (short for **noise vibration and harshness**)

DESIGN AND PERFORMANCE

ABBREVIATION **NVH** is the study of the noise and vibration levels of a vehicle.

○ *The automotive industry is changing as automakers learn more about controlling NVH.*

○ *Sounds making their way into the cab from outside were minimized by the carmaker's NVH control measures.*

Oo

---

oc|tane num|ber /ˈɒkteɪn nʌmbər/

NOUN **The octane number** of a fuel, especially gasoline, is a measure of its anti-knock properties.

- ○ *Gasoline characteristics that have an important effect on engines and emissions include its octane number and chemical composition.*
- ○ *Gasoline is classified by its research octane number (RON). In Britain standard unleaded gasoline is 95RON.*

> **MEASUREMENTS**
>
> Other measurements used in the automotive industry include:
>
> BHP, cetane number, horsepower, spring rate

---

o|dom|e|ter (In BRIT use **mileometer**) /oʊˈdɒmɪtər/ (**odometers**)

NOUN An **odometer** is a device in a vehicle which shows how far the vehicle has traveled.

- ○ *There were over 10,000 kilometers on the odometer.*
- ○ *Older vehicles with higher odometer readings will require a full service.*

> **WORD BUILDER**
> **-meter** = measuring device
>
> The suffix **-meter** is often used for devices that measure things:
> **chassis dynamometer**, **odometer**.

off-high|way ve|hi|cle /ɔf haɪweɪ viɪkᵊl/ (**off-highway vehicles**)

VEHICLE TYPES

NOUN An **off-highway vehicle** is a vehicle, such as one used for construction or agriculture, that is intended for use on steep or uneven ground.

○ Quad bikes and ATVs are examples of an off-highway vehicle.

○ An off-highway vehicle is any motor vehicle designed for or capable of cross-country travel.

oil gauge, oil gage or dipstick /ɔɪl geɪdʒ/ (**oil gauges**)

VEHICLE COMPONENTS: ENGINE, TRANSMISSION, AND EXHAUST

NOUN An **oil gauge** is a rod that shows the oil level in an engine oil pan or transmission.

○ There was plenty of gasoline, the oil gauge was registering pressure, yet the car was not heating up.

○ When I started the car I didn't get an oil reading on the oil gauge.

oil pan /ɔɪl pæn/ (**oil pans**)

VEHICLE COMPONENTS: ENGINE, TRANSMISSION, AND EXHAUST

NOUN An **oil pan** is the place under an engine that holds the engine oil.

○ He had already checked the oil pan for leakage and had seen none.

○ A vehicle's oil pan is a metal pan that is attached to the bottom of an engine's crankcase.

oil pump /ɔɪl pʌmp/ (**oil pumps**)

VEHICLE COMPONENTS: ENGINE, TRANSMISSION, AND EXHAUST

NOUN An **oil pump** is a pump that sends lubricating oil under pressure to the bearings and other lubricated surfaces of an engine.

○ The mechanic found small bits of metal in a valve in the oil pump.

○ The oil was kept clean by a pick-up screen inside the sump on the oil pump, and by an external filter.

Ot|to cy|cle /ɒtoʊ saɪkᵊl/

VEHICLE COMPONENTS: ENGINE, TRANSMISSION, AND EXHAUST

NOUN The **Otto cycle** is a cycle of engine operation which requires four strokes of the piston: for induction, compression, ignition, and exhaust. The fuel and air mixture is compressed before combustion is started by an electrical spark or other means. Named after German engineer Nikolaus Otto.

○ The reciprocating engine operates on the Otto cycle which is a constant volume cycle.

○ The Otto cycle is the dominant car-engine combustion process of the last century.

---

o|ver|drive /oʊvərdraɪv/ (**overdrives**)

VEHICLE COMPONENTS: ENGINE, TRANSMISSION, AND EXHAUST

NOUN The **overdrive** in a vehicle is a very high gear that is used when you are driving at high speeds.

○ The well-engineered gear ratios give it an overdrive in the fourth and fifth gears.

○ Fourth gear is needed for quick moves in traffic because fifth gear is an overdrive gear for relaxed highway cruising.

▶ **COLLOCATIONS:**
in overdrive
overdrive gear

---

o|ver|head valve /oʊvərhɛd vælv/ (**overhead valves**)

VEHICLE COMPONENTS: ENGINE, TRANSMISSION, AND EXHAUST

NOUN An **overhead valve** is a valve in the cylinder head of an engine.

○ He pressed the button on the starter motor and the overhead valve unit burst into life.

○ Modern racing cars are built with an overhead cam engine rather than an overhead valve engine.

o|ver|square en|gine /o͟uvərskwεər εndʒɪn/ (**oversquare engines**)

VEHICLE COMPONENTS: ENGINE, TRANSMISSION, AND EXHAUST

NOUN An **oversquare engine** is an engine which has a cylinder bore that is larger than its stroke.

○ *Generally, an oversquare engine will provide for high engine speeds, such as for automobile use.*

○ *An oversquare engine has the ability to spin faster because the shorter amount of ring travel reduces friction in the engine.*

o|ver|steer /o͟uvəstɪər/

DESIGN AND PERFORMANCE

NOUN **Oversteer** is the tendency of a vehicle to turn more sharply than expected.

○ *Oversteer can easily result in a spin.*

○ *With oversteer, the car turns more sharply than desired, taking a tighter line.*

Pp

pan|el /pǽnəl/ (panels)

VEHICLE COMPONENTS: BODYWORK, CONTROLS, AND ACCESSORIES

NOUN A **panel** is any section of sheet metal that forms part of a vehicle's bodywork, especially the outer part.

○ This car is better built, with thick steel panels and neat join lines between floorpan and body.

○ The collision caused damage to the roof and side panels of the car.

---

park¹ /pɑrk/

VEHICLE COMPONENTS: BRAKES, STEERING, WHEELS, TIRES, AND SUSPENSION

NOUN **Park** is a gear position on the automatic transmission of a vehicle that acts as a parking brake.

○ Place the shift lever in Park position.

○ The vehicle should be in Park while not running or while running but not moving for a period of time.

▶ COLLOCATION:
in park

---

park² /pɑrk/ (parks, parked, parking)

DESIGN AND PERFORMANCE

TRANSITIVE/INTRANSITIVE VERB When you **park** a vehicle or **park** somewhere, you drive the vehicle into a position where it can stay for a period of time, and leave it there.

○ He found a place to park the car.

○ There were only a few cars parked by the curb on one side of the road.

park|ing sen|sor /pɑrkɪŋ sɛnsər/ (parking sensors)

VEHICLE COMPONENTS: BODYWORK, CONTROLS, AND ACCESSORIES

NOUN A **parking sensor** is a device on a vehicle which detects obstacles and alerts the driver if the vehicle comes too close to them when being parked.

○ Because it is mounted on the rear bumper, a parking sensor is susceptible to damage.

○ The truck has an ultrasonic frontal impact parking sensor that detects obstacles.

par|tic|u|late fil|ter /pɑrtɪkyʊlɪt fɪltər/ (particulate filters)

VEHICLE COMPONENTS: ENGINE, TRANSMISSION, AND EXHAUST

NOUN A **particulate filter** is a filter to remove particles that are present in the air, for example in the exhaust of a diesel engine.

○ The use of diesel particulate filters has become popular as a way of meeting new emissions standards.

○ The engines are fitted with a particulate filter as standard for cleaner running.

pas|sen|ger car /pæsɪndʒər kɑr/ (passenger cars)

VEHICLE TYPES

NOUN A **passenger car** is any car designed for carrying fewer than ten people.

○ SUVs are more than three times more likely to roll over in a crash than a normal passenger car.

○ This was a vehicle designed to be a practical passenger car as well as a versatile cargo handler.

pas|sive re|straint /pæsɪv rɪstreɪnt/ (passive restraints)

VEHICLE COMPONENTS: BODYWORK, CONTROLS, AND ACCESSORIES

NOUN A **passive restraint** is any device, such as an air bag, that operates automatically to prevent you being thrown out of the seat of a vehicle if there is a crash.

○ *Passive restraints such as air bags or automatic seat belts are required in all vehicles.*

○ *The passive restraint rule required auto makers to install either air bags or automatically fastening seat belts.*

---

pe|dal /pɛdᵊl/ (pedals)

VEHICLE COMPONENTS: BODYWORK, CONTROLS, AND ACCESSORIES

NOUN A **pedal** in a vehicle is a lever that you press with your foot in order to control the vehicle.

○ *Her feet did not reach the brake or accelerator pedals.*

○ *The car has adjustable pedals for accelerator, brake, and clutch.*

---

per|for|mance /pərfɔrmᵊns/

DESIGN AND PERFORMANCE

NOUN A vehicle's **performance** is how well it operates.

○ *Advances have been made to improve the braking performance of commercial vehicles.*

○ *The vehicle had more power and better performance than any other car he had driven before.*

> **USAGE**
>
> Remember that this meaning of **performance** is uncountable. You cannot put *a* in front of it and you cannot make it plural.

---

pis|ton /pɪstᵊn/ (pistons)

VEHICLE COMPONENTS: ENGINE, TRANSMISSION, AND EXHAUST

NOUN A **piston** is a cylinder that is part of an engine. Pistons slide up and down inside tubes and cause various parts of the engine to move.

○ *As the pistons move up and down, the crank is rotated.*

○ *The reciprocating pistons are connected to the crankshaft by connecting rods.*

RELATED WORDS

A **piston** moves backward and forward in a **cylinder**.

A **connecting rod** connects a **crank** to a piston.

A **stroke** is one complete back-and-forth movement of a piston.

Dead center is the position of a piston at the very top or bottom of its stroke.

---

pis|ton land /pɪstᵊn lænd/ (**piston lands**)

VEHICLE COMPONENTS: ENGINE, TRANSMISSION, AND EXHAUST

NOUN A **piston land** is a raised area of a piston between piston rings.

○ *The flow of gas into the volume formed between the piston land between the first and second piston rings is limited by the top ring.*

○ *The air-fuel mixture trapped in the space between the piston land and the cylinder wall does not participate in the combustion process.*

---

pis|ton ring /pɪstᵊn rɪŋ/ (**piston rings**)

VEHICLE COMPONENTS: ENGINE, TRANSMISSION, AND EXHAUST

NOUN A **piston ring** is one of the rings, made of hard, springy material, that are part of a piston in an internal combustion engine.

○ *Shorter, lighter pistons with new piston ring surface treatment contribute to the increased horsepower and torque.*

○ *Engineers design the placement of the top piston ring to be as high as possible on the piston.*

---

pis|ton skirt /pɪstᵊn skɜrt/ (**piston skirts**)

VEHICLE COMPONENTS: ENGINE, TRANSMISSION, AND EXHAUST

NOUN The **piston skirt** is the cylindrical walls of a piston.

○ *During manufacture, the surface of the piston skirt is left slightly rough which helps retain lubrication.*

○ *The mixture travels up and around the piston skirt to reach the top piston ring.*

plain bear|ing /pleɪn bɛərɪŋ/ (**plain bearings**)

Vᴇʜɪᴄʟᴇ ᴄᴏᴍᴘᴏɴᴇɴᴛs: Eɴɢɪɴᴇ, ᴛʀᴀɴsᴍɪssɪᴏɴ, ᴀɴᴅ ᴇxʜᴀᴜsᴛ

NOUN A **plain bearing** is a shaft bearing in which a shaft rotates lubricated by an oil or grease.

○ *Plain bearings are not suitable for high-speed heavy loading situations.*

○ *In heavy-duty applications, the upper plain bearing is replaced by a tapered roller bearing that takes both radial and thrust loads.*

---

plan|e|tar|y trans|mis|sion /plænɪtɛri trænzmɪʃ°n/ (**planetary transmissions**)

Vᴇʜɪᴄʟᴇ ᴄᴏᴍᴘᴏɴᴇɴᴛs: Eɴɢɪɴᴇ, ᴛʀᴀɴsᴍɪssɪᴏɴ, ᴀɴᴅ ᴇxʜᴀᴜsᴛ

NOUN A **planetary transmission** is a special form of geared drive in which the input and output shafts are on the same axis.

○ *A three-phase motor drives the front wheels through a planetary transmission.*

○ *In planetary transmission, one gearwheel orbits around another.*

▶ **SYNONYM:**
epicyclic gearbox

> **TYPES OF TRANSMISSION INCLUDE:**
>
> automatic transmission, chain and sprocket drive, constant mesh gearbox, manual transmission, planetary transmission, synchromesh gearbox

---

plug¹ /plʌg/ (**plugs**)

Vᴇʜɪᴄʟᴇ ᴄᴏᴍᴘᴏɴᴇɴᴛs: Eɴɢɪɴᴇ, ᴛʀᴀɴsᴍɪssɪᴏɴ, ᴀɴᴅ ᴇxʜᴀᴜsᴛ

NOUN A **plug** is a cap that stops pressure from leaking or being lost, for example in the cooling system of a vehicle.

○ *The pressure plug is made to precision standards from alloy steel.*

○ *Since most manufacturers recommend periodic draining of the cooling system, and coolant changes, a plug is usually provided at the bottom of the radiator.*

plug² /plʌg/ (plugs)

VEHICLE COMPONENTS: ENGINE, TRANSMISSION, AND EXHAUST

NOUN A **plug** is a small plastic object with metal pins inside that is inserted into a socket to connect two electrical parts in a vehicle together, for example the engine and the instrument panel.

○ Before removing the car radio, remember to pull the plug out of the socket.

○ The two crocodile clips are attached to wires, with a switch and a two-point plug.

pneu|mat|ic tire (BRIT pneumatic tyre) /numǽtɪk taɪər/ (pneumatic tires)

VEHICLE COMPONENTS: BRAKES, STEERING, WHEELS, TIRES, AND SUSPENSION

NOUN A **pneumatic tire** is a rubber tire filled with air under pressure and mounted around the wheel of a vehicle.

○ The Michelin brothers proved the worth of pneumatic tires for early cars.

○ The outer part of the pneumatic tire is made of flexible, hollow rubber which is inflated by air pressure.

pol|lu|tant /pəlúːtᵊnt/ (pollutants)

FUELS, OILS, EMISSIONS, AND OTHER FLUIDS

NOUN **Pollutants** are substances that pollute the environment, especially gases from vehicles.

○ Among pollutants from vehicles, lead from gasoline engines has attracted most attention.

○ Children in strollers are more vulnerable than adults to attack from airborne pollutants such as exhaust fumes.

> **WORD BUILDER**
>
> **-ant** = causing
>
> The suffix **-ant** is used in words for substances that have a particular effect: **coolant**, **pollutant**.

pop|pet valve /pɒpɪt vælv/ (**poppet valves**)

VEHICLE COMPONENTS: ENGINE, TRANSMISSION, AND EXHAUST

NOUN A **poppet valve** is a disk-shaped intake or exhaust valve in an internal combustion engine.

○ *You can compress the valve diaphragm by hand to check if the poppet valve is functioning.*

○ *Each port is sealed off by a poppet valve.*

pow|er steer|ing /paʊər stɪərɪŋ/

VEHICLE COMPONENTS: BRAKES, STEERING, WHEELS, TIRES, AND SUSPENSION

NOUN In a vehicle, **power steering** or **power-assisted steering** is a system for steering that uses power from the engine so that it is easier for the driver to steer the vehicle.

○ *Nearly all power steering systems use fluid pressure to assist the driver in turning the front wheels.*

○ *The variable power steering, very light for parking, is firm at high speeds.*

pow|er win|dow (In BRIT use **electric window**) /paʊər wɪndoʊ/ (**power windows**)

VEHICLE COMPONENTS: BODYWORK, CONTROLS, AND ACCESSORIES

NOUN **Power windows** are windows in a vehicle which are raised or lowered by an electric motor operated by a button or switch.

○ *Power windows are opened and closed by drive motors.*

○ *Modern power windows have a switch on each door and a driver's master switch.*

pre|cham|ber /priːtʃeɪmbər/ (**prechambers**)

VEHICLE COMPONENTS: ENGINE, TRANSMISSION, AND EXHAUST

NOUN A **prechamber** in an engine is a small area, usually in the cylinder head, in which combustion is started before fuel enters into the main combustion chamber.

○ *The combustion chamber is divided into a prechamber and a main chamber.*

○ *Combustion begins in a small prechamber, then expands out into the cylinder.*

WORD BUILDER

pre- = before

The prefix **pre-** is often used in words connected with things that happen before something else: **prechamber**, **pre-ignition**.

---

pre-ig|ni|tion /priːˈɪgnɪʃən/

VEHICLE COMPONENTS: ENGINE, TRANSMISSION, AND EXHAUST

NOUN **Pre-ignition** is a situation in which the fuel-air mixture in a spark ignition engine ignites before the timed spark, because of contact with a hot surface.

○ *Over-heated spark plugs and exhaust valves are the main causes of pre-ignition.*

○ *Pre-ignition might be the consequence of the spark plug tip getting too hot.*

P|T|O /piː tiː ˈəʊ/ (short for **power take-off**)

VEHICLE COMPONENTS: ENGINE, TRANSMISSION, AND EXHAUST

ABBREVIATION A **PTO** is a shaft attached to the engine of a vehicle such as a truck or a tractor to which other equipment or machinery may be attached. The truck or tractor then provides the equipment or machinery with power.

○ *The PTO is a means of using the chassis engine to power accessories, eliminating the need for an additional auxiliary engine.*

○ *The PTO shaft on a tractor enables power to be delivered to stationary machines as well as to field machines.*

---

purge /pɜːrdʒ/ (**purges, purged, purging**)

FUELS, OILS, EMISSIONS, AND OTHER FLUIDS

VERB If you **purge** a fluid from a container or system, you drain and remove all traces of it.

○ *Usually, this system will purge all stored vapors in one trip.*

○ *Before reassembling the old farm tractor, they needed to purge its fuel tank to make sure it contained no sediment or rust.*

▶ **COLLOCATIONS:**
purge the system
purge the tank

Qq

quench /kwɛntʃ/ (**quenches, quenched, quenching**)

VERB If gases in the cylinder head are **quenched** during combustion in an internal combustion engine, a portion of them are cooled.

○ *One reason for flame quenching is the expansion of gases which takes place during combustion and power stroke.*

○ *The engine design team found that by having part of the piston crown almost touching the cylinder head at top dead center, detonation would be prevented. Because more heat would be lost over this area they called it "quench".*

▶ **COLLOCATION:**
quench gases

Rr

---

rack and pin|ion /ræk ənd pɪnyən/ (**rack and pinions**)

VEHICLE COMPONENTS: BRAKES, STEERING, WHEELS, TIRES, AND SUSPENSION

NOUN A **rack and pinion** is a type of steering gear in which a pinion on the end of the steering column engages with a horizontal rack (= flat-toothed bar).

○ *The speed-sensitive rack and pinion steering set-up was light and precise.*

○ *Many small cars use a rack and pinion steering system in which the steering wheel and shaft are connected to a small pinion gear.*

▶ **COLLOCATION:**
rack and pinion steering

---

ra|di|al ply tire (ABBR **radial**) /reɪdiəl plaɪ taɪər/ (**radial ply tires**)

VEHICLE COMPONENTS: BRAKES, STEERING, WHEELS, TIRES, AND SUSPENSION

NOUN A **radial ply tire** is a tire constructed on a base of layers of fabric that are laid radially (= coming from the same central point).

○ *Radial ply tires have a more flexible sidewall than bias ply tires.*

○ *A radial ply tire provides a larger tread contact patch than a comparable size bias ply tire.*

---

ra|di|a|tor /reɪdieɪtər/ (**radiators**)

VEHICLE COMPONENTS: ENGINE, TRANSMISSION, AND EXHAUST

NOUN The **radiator** in a vehicle is the part of the engine that is filled with water in order to cool the engine.

○ *Car radiator failures are usually caused by loss of cooling water from breaks in the rubber tubing rather than fracture of the reservoir.*

○ *If the coolant needs refilling, make sure to wait until the engine and radiator are cold.*

---

rear|view mir|ror /rɪərvyu mɪrər/ (**rearview mirrors**)

VEHICLE COMPONENTS: BODYWORK, CONTROLS, AND ACCESSORIES

NOUN Inside a car, the **rearview mirror** is the mirror that allows you to see the traffic behind when you are driving.

○ *She saw the reflection of a pair of headlamps in the rearview mirror.*

○ *He forgot to check his rearview mirror when he backed out of the parking space.*

---

re|cip|ro|cat|ing en|gine /rɪsɪprəkeɪtɪŋ ɛndʒɪn/ (**reciprocating engines**)

VEHICLE COMPONENTS: ENGINE, TRANSMISSION, AND EXHAUST

NOUN A **reciprocating engine** is an engine in which a piston is moved up and down in a cylinder by a mechanism such as a crankshaft and connecting rod.

○ *The moving piston controls the volume of the combustion chamber in a reciprocating engine.*

○ *A reciprocating engine has pistons moving back and forth inside.*

---

re|gen|er|a|tive brak|ing /rɪdʒɛnərətɪv breɪkɪŋ/

VEHICLE COMPONENTS: BRAKES, STEERING, WHEELS, TIRES, AND SUSPENSION

NOUN **Regenerative braking** is a form of braking in electric vehicles in which the loss of kinetic energy from braking is stored and then fed back later to provide power to the electric motor.

○ *The system uses regenerative braking to recharge the battery.*

○ *Power comes from an eight-horsepower electric motor and energy is also recaptured through regenerative braking on all four wheels.*

---

re|lay /rɪleɪ/ (**relays**)

VEHICLE COMPONENTS: LIGHTING AND ELECTRICAL/ELECTRONIC SYSTEMS

NOUN A **relay** is a usually electrical device that switches on in response to a physical change, such as a pressure change or temperature change.

○ Almost all modern cars use relays to switch the headlamps and avoid the need to route their full current through the lighting switches.

○ There are two fuses and a relay that could keep the fuel pump from running.

---

re|tread|ed tire /rɪtrɛdɪd taɪər/ (**retreaded tires**)

VEHICLE COMPONENTS: BRAKES, STEERING, WHEELS, TIRES, AND SUSPENSION

NOUN A **retreaded tire** is a used tire with a new tread fixed to it.

○ Retreaded tires nowadays can at least equal the mileage of a new tire.

○ Not removing enough old tread causes problems because the retreaded tire will not have enough clean rubber to adhere to.

---

re|verse¹ /rɪvɜrs/

DESIGN AND PERFORMANCE

NOUN If your car is **in reverse**, you have changed gears so that you can drive it backward.

○ Tom put the car in reverse and backed out of the garage.

○ She put the car in reverse by mistake and damaged a car parked behind her.

▶ COLLOCATION:
  in reverse

---

re|verse² /rɪvɜrs/ (**reverses, reversed, reversing**)

DESIGN AND PERFORMANCE

TRANSITIVE/INTRANSITIVE VERB When a car **reverses**, or when you **reverse** it, the car is driven backward.

○ She had to reverse the car out of the parking space.

○ He started the car, and reversed back out into the lane.

---

rich mix|ture /rɪtʃ mɪkstʃər/ (**rich mixtures**)

FUELS, OILS, EMISSIONS, AND OTHER FLUIDS

NOUN A **rich mixture** is a fuel/air mixture containing an excessive proportion of fuel.

○A rich mixture may be desirable under certain operating conditions, such as when the engine is under load.

○A rich mixture provides enough fuel to use up all of the oxygen in the cylinder.

---

ride /raɪd/

DESIGN AND PERFORMANCE

NOUN The **ride** of a vehicle is how well it works on uneven ground, in particular how well the suspension system operates to make traveling inside comfortable.

○The car has superb handling, a comfortable ride, and acres of room.

○The new truck air suspension system provides excellent roll stability without compromising the soft ride characteristics of air suspension.

---

rim /rɪm/ (**rims**)

VEHICLE COMPONENTS: BRAKES, STEERING, WHEELS, TIRES, AND SUSPENSION; ENGINE, TRANSMISSION, AND EXHAUST

NOUN The **rim** of a wheel is its outside edge, on which the tire is mounted.

○The car's clean and handsome body sits on 17-inch rims with steel wheels.

○Water seems to seep down between the tire and rim where it corrodes the aluminum.

---

road|hold|ing /roʊdhoʊldɪŋ/

DESIGN AND PERFORMANCE

NOUN **Roadholding** is a term that people use to talk about how well a vehicle responds to being driven and how easy it is to control.

○The vehicle's roadholding was much better than I expected and the ride was superb.

○It is a popular sports car, with a low center of gravity and excellent performance and roadholding.

rock|er arm /rɒkər ɑrm/ (**rocker arms**)

NOUN A **rocker arm** is a centrally pivoted lever in the valve train of an engine that converts the motion of the rods to open the valves.

○ *Rocker arms transmit motion from the cam lobes to the valves.*

○ *One end of each rocker arm carries an adjusting screw with a cap or cup which is in contact with the push rod.*

roll cage /roʊl keɪdʒ/ (**roll cages**)

NOUN A **roll cage** is a safety structure built onto an open car, tractor, or off-highway vehicle to protect the people inside if the vehicle rolls over.

○ *The burnt wreck of the car showed how the steel roll cage helped save their lives.*

○ *The bodyshell of the rally car is stiffened and incorporates a roll cage.*

roll cen|ter /roʊl sɛntər/ (**roll centers**)

NOUN The **roll center** is the center about which a vehicle body rolls.

○ *Handling is said to be enhanced with a lower roll center for the front suspension.*

○ *The roll center is the imaginary point where the wheels pivot inward as the suspension moves up and down during heavy cornering loads.*

roll|er chain /roʊlər tʃeɪn/ (**roller chains**)

NOUN A **roller chain** is a chain in which hard steel rollers engage with the sprocket wheels.

○ *They used a phased roller chain drive, with three chains, as the input for a manual transmission.*

○ *A double roller chain operated the cams.*

roll|ing road /ˈroʊlɪŋ roʊd/ (**rolling roads**)

<u>DESIGN AND PERFORMANCE</u>

NOUN A **rolling road** is a piece of machinery on which the wheels of a vehicle can ride in order to test how well the vehicle works under road conditions that are created artificially.

  ○ Fuel efficiency figures are obtained from simple tests at different speeds on a rolling road.

  ○ Final tuning should only be done by an experienced operator on a dynamometer or a rolling road.

roof pan|el /ruf pænᵊl/ (**roof panels**)

<u>VEHICLE COMPONENTS: BODYWORK, CONTROLS, AND ACCESSORIES</u>

NOUN The **roof panel** is the section of material, usually sheet metal, that forms the roof of a vehicle.

  ○ Its long, low hood was impressive, as was the flat roof panel.

  ○ The roof is split into three sections – the aluminum roof panel, the strengthened C pillars, and the rear windshield.

ro|tor arm /ˈroʊtər ɑrm/ (**rotor arms**)

<u>VEHICLE COMPONENTS: ENGINE, TRANSMISSION, AND EXHAUST</u>

NOUN The **rotor arm** is the rotating electrical high-tension contact of the distributor in a spark ignition engine.

  ○ Lift off the distributor cap and take out the rotor arm.

  ○ The rotor arm should be pointing at a notch in the distributor body rim.

rub|ber /ˈrʌbər/

<u>MATERIALS</u>

NOUN **Rubber** is a strong, waterproof, elastic substance made from the juice of a tropical tree or produced chemically. It is used for making tires.

  ○ This is a recycled tire which has had its worn tread rubber replaced with new tread.

  ○ Heat and pressure is used to vulcanize the rubber and create a new tread design.

Ss

---

safe|ty cage /ˈseɪfti keɪdʒ/ (safety cages)

NOUN A **safety cage** is a rigid part of the body of a vehicle that surrounds the passenger compartment and protects passengers during a crash.

○ *The body of the car needs to be assembled around the safety cage.*

○ *This model has been extensively crash-tested, and boasts a tough steel safety cage and energy absorbing bumpers.*

> **OTHER VEHICLE PARTS THAT PROTECT PASSENGERS INCLUDE:**
>
> air bag, bull bars, bumper, roll cage, side impact bar

---

sat|el|lite nav|i|ga|tion sys|tem (ABBR **sat nav**) /ˈsætəlaɪt nævɪˈɡeɪʃən sɪstəm/ (satellite navigation systems)

NOUN A **satellite navigation system** is a computer-operated system in a vehicle that uses satellites to show the driver the position of the vehicle and which way it should travel to reach its destination.

○ *The satellite navigation system is integrated into the car and has been preset with the legal speed limit on the roads.*

○ *The system includes a satellite navigation system and monitor to show a map and provide directions.*

scav|eng|ing /skævəndʒɪŋ/

VEHICLE COMPONENTS: ENGINE, TRANSMISSION, AND EXHAUST

NOUN **Scavenging** is the removal of exhaust gases from an engine cylinder.

○ *A part of the compressed air can be easily diverted to ensure complete scavenging of the exhaust gases.*

○ *Scavenging is the process by which exhaust gases are expelled from the combustion chamber and fresh charge is introduced.*

scut|tle /skʌtᵊl/ (**scuttles**)

VEHICLE COMPONENTS: BODYWORK, CONTROLS, AND ACCESSORIES

NOUN The **scuttle** is the lower, forward part of a driver's cab or passenger compartment that provides space for the legs of people in the car and separates them from the engine compartment.

○ *The inner structure was strong, but the scuttle had been solidly welded half an inch too far to the left.*

○ *The wiper motor was mounted on the left-hand side under the scuttle.*

seat¹ /siːt/ (**seats**)

DESIGN AND PERFORMANCE

NOUN A **seat** is the support and attachment point for a load-carrying part in a vehicle, for example a spring seat.

○ *An insulator is located between the lower spring seat and the bottom of the coil spring.*

○ *The seat for the front suspension coil springs must be secure otherwise steering would become dangerous.*

seat² /siːt/ (**seats**)

VEHICLE COMPONENTS: BODYWORK, CONTROLS, AND ACCESSORIES

NOUN A **seat** in a vehicle is the chair that the driver or passenger sits on.

○ *The front seat is on slides, with a reclining backrest.*

○ *He opened the car door and eased himself into the driver's seat.*

s

▶ COLLOCATIONS:
back seat
driver's seat
front seat
passenger seat

---

seat belt (ABBR belt) /sit bɛlt/ (seat belts)

VEHICLE COMPONENTS: BODYWORK, CONTROLS, AND ACCESSORIES

NOUN A **seat belt** is a strap attached to a seat in a vehicle. You fasten it across your body in order to prevent yourself being thrown out of the seat if there is a sudden movement or stop.

○ *She got into the car and fastened her seat belt.*

○ *The fact that he was wearing a seat belt saved his life.*

---

seat belt ten|sion|er /sit bɛlt tɛnʃənər/ (seat belt tensioners)

VEHICLE COMPONENTS: BODYWORK, CONTROLS, AND ACCESSORIES

NOUN A **seat belt tensioner** is a device in a vehicle that pulls a seat belt tight if there is a sudden movement or stop.

○ *Standard safety features include a driver's air bag and seat belt tensioners.*

○ *A seat belt tensioner considerably increases the passenger protection afforded by the safety belts in the case of an accident.*

---

sem|i|trail|er /sɛmitreɪlər/ (semitrailers)

VEHICLE TYPES

NOUN A **semitrailer** is the long rear section of a truck that can bend when it turns.

○ *The truck driver was slightly injured when his semitrailer overturned.*

○ *Heavy trucks and semitrailers account for about 15 percent of all traffic along the highway, yet make up 25 percent of all vehicles involved in fatal crashes.*

ser|vo-mech|a|nism /sɜrvou mɛkənɪzəm/ (**servo-mechanisms**)

VEHICLE COMPONENTS: BODYWORK, CONTROLS, AND ACCESSORIES

NOUN A **servo-mechanism** is a system or device that provides increased power to operate a control.

○ *The electromechanical servo-mechanism is designed to collect an exhaust sample at a rate that is proportional to engine airflow.*

○ *Any mechanism which adds to the efforts of the driver in applying the brakes is called a servo-mechanism.*

shock ab|sorb|er /ʃɒk əbsɔrbər/ (**shock absorbers**)

VEHICLE COMPONENTS: ENGINE, TRANSMISSION, AND EXHAUST

NOUN A **shock absorber** is a device fitted near the wheels of a vehicle to reduce the effects of traveling over uneven ground.

○ *The car is fitted with a pair of rear shock absorbers.*

○ *The shock absorber's function is to control, or damp, all bounce.*

side im|pact bar /saɪd ɪmpækt bɑr/ (**side impact bars**)

VEHICLE COMPONENTS: BODYWORK, CONTROLS, AND ACCESSORIES

NOUN A **side impact bar** is a long beam in a car door that is designed to protect passengers during a crash.

○ *Side impact bars and side air bags may reduce injury.*

○ *The inner skin of a car door usually has stiffening ribs for strength and may also contain a side impact bar.*

S

sill /sɪl/ (**sills**)

VEHICLE COMPONENTS: BODYWORK, CONTROLS, AND ACCESSORIES

NOUN The **sill** is the strong horizontal part at the side of the floor of a vehicle onto which a door closes.

○ *The sill runs between the front and rear wheel arches below the door.*

○ *Some car doors overlap, and hide, their sills.*

skid /skɪd/ (**skids, skidded, skidding**)

DESIGN AND PERFORMANCE

VERB If a vehicle **skids**, it slides sideways or forward while moving, for example when you are trying to stop it suddenly on a wet road.

○ *The car pulled up too fast and skidded on the dusty shoulder of the road.*

○ *She wrenched the steering wheel straight and the car skidded on the damp roadway for some distance.*

---

skirt /skɜrt/ (**skirts**)

VEHICLE COMPONENTS: BODYWORK, CONTROLS, AND ACCESSORIES

NOUN The **skirt** of a vehicle's bodywork is any part that extends downward to cover or protect the wheels or underside of the vehicle.

○ *On the skirt of the car, there was a reflective stripe.*

○ *Extending the skirt downwards may indeed reduce the drag, but it will also reduce the ground clearance on uneven tracks.*

---

sleeve /sliv/ (**sleeves**)

VEHICLE COMPONENTS: ENGINE, TRANSMISSION, AND EXHAUST

NOUN The **sleeve** of an engine cylinder is its hard metal lining.

○ *The cylinders used replaceable sleeves to avoid costly rebores if the engine needs to be reconditioned.*

○ *With the cylinder head removed, the bores can be checked for size and whether or not the block has a sleeve or sleeves.*

---

snub|ber /snʌbər/ (**snubbers**)

VEHICLE COMPONENTS: BRAKES, STEERING, WHEELS, TIRES, AND SUSPENSION

NOUN A **snubber** is a rubber or metal spring device on a vehicle that limits the movement of a mechanism and at the same time acts as a shock absorber and prevents sudden stops.

○ *A rubber snubber in the trunk panel holds the panels at the correct height.*

○ *The road was so uneven that the axle was often striking the snubbers.*

soft top /sɒft tɒp/ (**soft tops**)

VEHICLE TYPES

NOUN A **soft top** is a vehicle with a soft roof that can sometimes be folded down or removed.

○ *The coupe comes in a hard top model and a version with a fold-away soft top.*

○ *She drives a two-seater soft top in the summer, with the roof rolled down.*

so|le|noid switch /sɒulənɔɪd swɪtʃ/ (**solenoid switches**)

VEHICLE COMPONENTS: LIGHTING AND ELECTRICAL/ELECTRONIC SYSTEMS

NOUN A **solenoid switch** is an electrical switch that is often used where a high current circuit, such as a starter motor circuit, is brought into operation by a low current switch.

○ *When the key switch is turned to Start and the gearshift is in neutral, the circuit between the battery and the solenoid switch is complete.*

○ *The solenoid switch activates a heavy-duty switch that connects the vehicle's battery to the starter motor.*

spare wheel /spɛər wiːl/ (**spare wheels**)

VEHICLE COMPONENTS: BODYWORK, CONTROLS, AND ACCESSORIES

NOUN A **spare wheel** is a wheel that you keep in your car in case you get a flat tire and need to replace one of your wheels.

○ *Observe the speed restrictions marked on the spare wheel while it is in place, and get the punctured tire fixed as soon as possible.*

○ *Luggage space with all the seats up is quite restricted, even with the spare wheel mounted externally.*

spark ig|ni|tion en|gine[1] (ABBR **SI engine**) /spɑrk ɪgnɪʃⁿn ɛndʒɪn/ (**spark ignition engines**)

VEHICLE COMPONENTS: ENGINE, TRANSMISSION, AND EXHAUST

NOUN A **spark ignition engine** is an engine running on the Otto cycle.

○ *A four-stroke spark ignition engine is an Otto cycle engine.*

○ *Direct injection technology increases the torque and power of spark ignition engines and makes them 15 percent more economical.*

spark ig|ni|tion en|gine² (ABBR **SI engine**) /spɑrk ɪgnɪʃⁿn ɛndʒɪn/ (**spark ignition engines**)

VEHICLE COMPONENTS: ENGINE, TRANSMISSION, AND EXHAUST

NOUN A **spark ignition engine** is any form of reciprocating engine in which combustion is started by a spark.

- ○ Is it a spark ignition engine or a compression ignition engine?
- ○ There has been a 10 percent increase in the customs duty on the components of spark ignition engines and compression ignition engines.

spark plug or sparking plug /spɑrk plʌg/ (**spark plugs**)

VEHICLE COMPONENTS: ENGINE, TRANSMISSION, AND EXHAUST

NOUN A **spark plug** is a device in the engine of a vehicle which produces electric sparks to make the gasoline burn.

- ○ It's a diesel engine, so it doesn't have a spark plug.
- ○ When the piston reaches the top of its stroke, the spark plug emits a spark to ignite the fuel.

spe|cif|ic fuel con|sump|tion (ABBR **SFC**) /spɪsɪfɪk fyuəl kənsʌmpʃⁿn/

DESIGN AND PERFORMANCE

NOUN **Specific fuel consumption** is the amount of fuel consumed by a vehicle for each unit of power output.

- ○ A vehicle's specific fuel consumption is more or less independent from its nitrogen oxide emissions per kilometer.
- ○ The specific fuel consumption of an engine is the rate of fuel burnt to produce a unit of thrust.

spoil|er /spɔɪlər/ (**spoilers**)

VEHICLE COMPONENTS: BODYWORK, CONTROLS, AND ACCESSORIES

NOUN A **spoiler** is an object which forms part of the body of a vehicle. It changes the flow of air around the vehicle, making forward movement more efficient.

- ○ The overall body shape, front spoiler, and door mirrors have all been modified to maximize the car's performance.

○ *The spoiler, which is attached on the trunk, collects air as it flows over the vehicle, and the air forces the back end into the ground, making it more stable.*

▶ COLLOCATIONS:
front spoiler
rear spoiler

---

spring rate /sprɪŋ reɪt/ (**spring rates**)
DESIGN AND PERFORMANCE

NOUN The **spring rate** is a measurement of the amount of force needed to compress a spring a particular distance.

○ *The spring rate was measured by loading the tractor with a certain sprung mass.*

○ *Engineers have been working to find the optimum spring rate for the front and rear suspension.*

---

sta|bi|li|zer bar (In BRIT use **anti-roll bar**) /steɪbɪlaɪzər bɑːr/ (**stabilizer bars**)
VEHICLE COMPONENTS: ENGINE, TRANSMISSION, AND EXHAUST

NOUN A **stabilizer bar** is a torsion bar that joins the nearside (= on the side near the pavement) and offside (= on the side away from the pavement) wheel suspensions of an independent suspension system, intended to reduce the amount that the vehicle body rolls.

○ *The front suspension arrangement is an independent setup with coil springs and a stabilizer bar.*

○ *The stabilizer bar connects one side of the suspension to the other through the frame.*

---

stain|less steel /steɪnlɪs stiːl/
MATERIALS

NOUN **Stainless steel** is a metal made from steel and chromium which does not rust.

○ *The car will have handmade stainless steel trim.*

○ *The manufacturer has installed stainless steel rivets to strengthen both sides of the car.*

stall /stɔl/ (**stalls, stalled, stalling**)

DESIGN AND PERFORMANCE

INTRANSITIVE/TRANSITIVE VERB If a vehicle **stalls** or if you accidentally **stall** it, the engine stops suddenly.

○ *She slammed on the brakes and the engine stalled.*

○ *The engine stalled and he saw that the fuel gauge needle hovered over empty.*

start|er mo|tor (INFORMAL **cranking motor**) /stɑrtər moutər/ (**starter motors**)

VEHICLE COMPONENTS: ENGINE, TRANSMISSION, AND EXHAUST

NOUN A **starter motor** is an electric motor for starting an engine.

○ *The starter motor needs a lot of current because of the amount of energy required to turn over the engine.*

○ *When an engine is cranked, the heavy draw of the starter motor temporarily pulls down the battery voltage.*

steel /stil/

MATERIALS

NOUN **Steel** is a very strong metal which is made mainly from iron. Steel is used for making vehicles.

○ *Sheet steel is pressed into the shapes of the various panels of the car and welded together.*

○ *The vehicle is very well-built with thick steel panels and neat join lines between floorpan and body.*

steer|ing col|umn /stɪərɪŋ kɒləm/ (**steering columns**)

VEHICLE COMPONENTS: BODYWORK, CONTROLS, AND ACCESSORIES

NOUN The **steering column** of a vehicle is the rod to which the steering wheel is attached.

○ *The steering wheel is mounted on a shaft inside the steering column.*

○ *The steering column carries the steering inputs to the steering rack or box.*

steer|ing ge|om|e|try /stɪərɪŋ dʒɪɒmɪtri/

DESIGN AND PERFORMANCE

NOUN **Steering geometry** is the geometric arrangement of the parts of a steering system, and the value of the lengths and angles within it.

○ *The rack and pinion steering had to be re-sited and that ruined the steering geometry.*

○ *Steering geometry changes due to bumps in the road may cause the front wheels to steer in a different direction together or independent of each other.*

steer|ing wheel (ABBR **wheel**) /stɪərɪŋ wil/ (**steering wheels**)

VEHICLE COMPONENTS: BODYWORK, CONTROLS, AND ACCESSORIES

NOUN The **steering wheel** of a vehicle is the wheel which the driver holds when he or she is driving.

○ *The wheels on the car turn 20 degrees during one rotation of the steering wheel.*

○ *The front wheels are steered via rods connected to the steering wheel.*

stick shift /stɪk ʃɪft/ (**stick shifts**)

VEHICLE COMPONENTS: BODYWORK, CONTROLS, AND ACCESSORIES

NOUN A **stick shift** is the lever that you use to change gear in a vehicle.

○ *The customer can choose between stick shift and automatic transmission and between mechanical and power steering.*

○ *She eased the stick shift into neutral.*

stoi|chi|o|met|ric ra|ti|o /stɔɪkiəmɛtrɪk reɪʃoʊ/ (**stoichiometric ratios**)

DESIGN AND PERFORMANCE

NOUN The **stoichiometric ratio** is the exact ratio between air and flammable gas or vapor at which complete combustion takes place.

○ *The stoichiometric ratio of combustion varies for various fuels and oxidizers.*

○ *If the engine has less air than the stoichiometric ratio, you have a rich mixture, because it is rich in gasoline.*

PRONUNCIATION

Note that the "ch" in "stoichiometric" is pronounced "k."
There are several types of ratio that are used in automotive
engineering. Make sure you put the stress on the right syllable.

air-fuel ratio /ɛər fyuəl reɪʃoʊ/
bore-stroke ratio /bɔr stroʊk reɪʃoʊ/
compression ratio /kəmprɛʃᵊn reɪʃoʊ/
gear ratio /gɪər reɪʃoʊ/
stoichiometric ratio /stɔɪkiəmɛtrɪk reɪʃoʊ/

---

stroke /stroʊk/ (strokes)

VEHICLE COMPONENTS: ENGINE, TRANSMISSION, AND EXHAUST

NOUN A **stroke** is one complete back-and-forth movement of a piston in
its cylinder bore.

○ *There are four valves per cylinder, and the stroke is longer than most other
engines.*

○ *A very small distance normally exists between exhaust valves and pistons
when they are at the top of their stroke.*

---

sun|roof /sʌnruf/ (sunroofs)

VEHICLE COMPONENTS: BODYWORK, CONTROLS, AND ACCESSORIES

NOUN A **sunroof** is a panel in the roof of a vehicle that opens to let
sunshine and air enter the car.

○ *The sunroof is opened by an electric motor actuated by a switch on the
dashboard.*

○ *The feeling of spaciousness in the car is heightened by the all-glass full-length
sunroof.*

---

su|per|char|ger /supərtʃɑrdʒər/ (superchargers)

VEHICLE COMPONENTS: ENGINE, TRANSMISSION, AND EXHAUST

NOUN A **supercharger** is a mechanical pump or compressor for
increasing the pressure of air or gases that are drawn into an engine.

○ *A supercharger provides the necessary push when the car needs it.*

○ *The car's performance is superb, and it provides the seamless acceleration possible with a supercharger.*

---

sus|pen|sion /səspɛnʃᵊn/ (**suspensions**)

VEHICLE COMPONENTS: BRAKES, STEERING, WHEELS, TIRES, AND SUSPENSION

NOUN A vehicle's **suspension** consists of the springs and other devices attached to the wheels, which give a smooth ride over uneven ground.

○ *This is the only small car that they make with independent front suspension.*

○ *The ride of the car felt better with its suspension lowered, but it was still over-geared.*

▶ **COLLOCATIONS:**
front suspension
rear suspension

> **THE SUSPENSION CAN INCLUDE:**
>
> A-arm, damper, stabilizer bar, torsion bar, trailing arm

---

sus|pen|sion ge|om|e|try /səspɛnʃᵊn dʒiɒmɪtri/

DESIGN AND PERFORMANCE

NOUN **Suspension geometry** is the geometric arrangement of the parts of a suspension system, and the value of the lengths and angles within it.

○ *They say they have sharpened the car's on-road performance with revised suspension geometry.*

○ *If your car's steering has even a mild pull to one side, it is probable that the suspension geometry is askew.*

---

syn|chro|mesh gear|box /sɪŋkroumɛʃ gɪərbɒks/ (**syncromesh gearboxes**)

VEHICLE COMPONENTS: ENGINE, TRANSMISSION, AND EXHAUST

NOUN A **synchromesh gearbox** is a usually manually operated transmission in which a change of gears takes place between gears that are already revolving at the same speed.

s

○ *It is often claimed that a synchromesh gearbox requires less effort to change gears.*

○ *Before the synchromesh gearbox was introduced in the 1930s, every driver had to master the difficult task of double-declutching.*

S

Tt

tail|gate /teɪlɡeɪt/ (tailgates)

VEHICLE COMPONENTS: BODYWORK, CONTROLS, AND ACCESSORIES

NOUN A **tailgate** is a door at the back of a vehicle that is hinged at the bottom so that it opens downward.

○ He put up the tailgate of the truck, locking it into place.

○ Aluminum hoods, fenders, and tailgates are increasingly evident on trucks, which need the most help meeting fuel-economy targets.

tap|pet /tæpɪt/ (tappets)

VEHICLE COMPONENTS: ENGINE, TRANSMISSION, AND EXHAUST

NOUN A **tappet** is the part of an engine gear train that converts cam lift into linear reciprocating (= up and down) movement which it transmits to the valve.

○ Problems with hydraulic tappets can be caused by dirty oil blocking the fine filters.

○ The tappet is the mechanism which lifts the valve, which is adjustable in most modern cars.

ter|mi|nal post /tɜrmɪnəl poʊst/ (terminal posts)

VEHICLE COMPONENTS: LIGHTING AND ELECTRICAL/ELECTRONIC SYSTEMS

NOUN A **terminal post** is the terminal on a battery to which the battery lead is attached.

○ Remove the nut from the battery bolt, and lift the battery cable connection off the negative terminal post.

○ Once disconnected, make sure the negative terminal clamp cannot swing back onto its terminal post.

throt|tle /ˈθrɒtᵊl/ (throttles)

VEHICLE COMPONENTS: ENGINE, TRANSMISSION, AND EXHAUST

NOUN The **throttle** of a vehicle is the device, lever, or pedal that controls the quantity of fuel entering the engine and is used to control the vehicle's speed.

○ *The engine slows down quickly when you lift your foot from the throttle.*

○ *To get top performance out of this car, you really need to press the throttle right to the floor.*

> **TALKING ABOUT USING THE THROTTLE**
>
> You can say that you **push** the throttle into a particular position, or if you move it in a gentle way, you **ease** it forward or back.
>
> If you **open** the throttle, you let more fuel into the engine.
>
> If a vehicle is operating **at full throttle**, the throttle is letting in as much fuel as possible.

thrust bear|ing /ˈθrʌst ˌbɛərɪŋ/ (thrust bearings)

VEHICLE COMPONENTS: ENGINE, TRANSMISSION, AND EXHAUST

NOUN A **thrust bearing** is a bearing which allows parts to rotate with little friction whilst absorbing an axial thrust.

○ *The single plate dry clutch, with ball thrust bearing, is assembled with the engine and three-speed gearbox.*

○ *A thrust bearing must be used to control end thrust.*

tick o|ver /ˈtɪk ˌoʊvər/ (ticks over, ticked over, ticking over)

DESIGN AND PERFORMANCE

VERB If an engine is **ticking over**, it is running at a low speed without moving.

○ *He left his car engine ticking over while he cleaned the windshield.*

○ *It is a good idea to let the engine tick over for 30–45 seconds to allow oil to circulate through the top of the engine.*

tim|ing /taɪmɪŋ/

VEHICLE COMPONENTS: ENGINE, TRANSMISSION, AND EXHAUST

NOUN **Timing** is used to refer to the time at which processes related to an engine's operating cycle happen, or to the length of time that they take.

○ *Torque control is realized by a combination of ignition timing and injection cut-out.*

○ *An engine with too much timing will detonate, regardless of how much fuel it receives.*

tim|ing belt /taɪmɪŋ bɛlt/ (**timing belts**)

VEHICLE COMPONENTS: ENGINE, TRANSMISSION, AND EXHAUST

NOUN A **timing belt** is a flat-toothed belt that drives the camshaft of an engine from the crankshaft.

○ *Her car has just broken a camshaft timing belt.*

○ *The timing belt is important to the camshaft and crankshaft. It keeps the motor in time.*

tim|ing chain /taɪmɪŋ tʃeɪn/ (**timing chains**)

VEHICLE COMPONENTS: ENGINE, TRANSMISSION, AND EXHAUST

NOUN A **timing chain** is a continuous roller chain that drives the camshaft of an engine from the crankshaft.

○ *As an engine ages, its timing chain stretches.*

○ *Larger cars and trucks connect the camshaft and crankshaft with a timing chain rather than a timing belt.*

tire /taɪər/ (**tires**)

VEHICLE COMPONENTS: BRAKES, STEERING, WHEELS, TIRES, AND SUSPENSION

NOUN A **tire** is a thick piece of rubber which is fitted onto the wheels of a vehicle.

○ *In the trunk was a spare tire and a jack.*

○ *An underinflated tire causes a wheel to turn slightly faster than the others.*

> **TYPES OF TIRE INCLUDE:**
>
> bias ply tire, pneumatic tire, radial ply tire, retreaded tire

---

toe-in /toʊ ɪn/

DESIGN AND PERFORMANCE

NOUN **Toe-in** describes the setting of a pair of wheels on an axle in which the edge of each wheel is inclined slightly inward.

○ *The multi-link rear suspension seems to work well, with a certain amount of automatic toe-in adjustment.*

○ *A small amount of toe-in will make the car more stable on a straight road but just a bit less responsive turning into the corners.*

---

toe-out /toʊ aʊt/

DESIGN AND PERFORMANCE

NOUN **Toe-out** describes the setting of a pair of wheels on an axle in which the edge of each wheel is inclined slightly outward.

○ *The track rod and steering arm were bent, giving the front wheels 2½ inches toe-out.*

○ *Toe-out encourages the initiation of a turn, while toe-in discourages it.*

---

top dead cen|ter (ABBR **TDC**) /tɒp dɛd sɛntər/

VEHICLE COMPONENTS: ENGINE, TRANSMISSION, AND EXHAUST

NOUN **Top dead center** is the position of an engine's piston when it is at the very top of its stroke.

○ *The piston has moved up towards the top dead center.*

○ *The piston is said to be at top dead center when it has moved to a position where the cylinder volume is a minimum.*

---

torque con|vert|er /tɔrk kənvɜrtər/ (**torque converters**)

VEHICLE COMPONENTS: ENGINE, TRANSMISSION, AND EXHAUST

NOUN A **torque converter** is a device that transmits torque (= twisting force) from one shaft to another.

○ *The torque converter is generally used with automatic transmissions, where it serves as a hydraulic clutch.*

○ *The torque converter gives the car more torque when it accelerates out of a stop.*

PRONUNCIATION

Note that **torque** only has one syllable. It comes from the Latin *torquere*, which means "to twist."

---

tor|sion bar /tɔrʃᵊn bɑr/ (torsion bars)

VEHICLE COMPONENTS: BRAKES, STEERING, WHEELS, TIRES, AND SUSPENSION

NOUN A **torsion bar** is a bar attached to a vehicle's suspension that absorbs energy by twisting.

○ *Torsion bar front suspension systems are often used on four-wheel-drive trucks.*

○ *The car's basic torsion bar suspension was lowered to improve handling and a front anti-sway bar fitted.*

---

track-lay|ing ve|hi|cle (INFORMAL crawler) /træk leɪɪŋ viɪkᵊl/ (track-laying vehicles)

VEHICLE TYPES

NOUN A **track-laying vehicle** is a vehicle whose wheels run inside a continuous chain or track.

○ *A track-laying vehicle could be described as a wheeled vehicle carrying its own road.*

○ *With a track-laying vehicle, the engine drives small cogwheels that run along the top of the track in contact with the ground.*

---

track rod /træk rɒd/ (track rods)

VEHICLE COMPONENTS: BRAKES, STEERING, WHEELS, TIRES, AND SUSPENSION

NOUN A **track rod** is a rod that connects the steering arms of steered wheels.

○ *The track rod and steering arm of the car were bent.*

○ *The rack is jointed to the wheel hubs by two track rods.*

trac|tion /trækʃən/

DESIGN AND PERFORMANCE

NOUN **Traction** is the grip that the wheels of a vehicle have on the ground.

○ The car began to skid as the wheels lost traction.

○ They deflated their tires slightly to increase traction where the sand was soft.

trac|tion con|trol /trækʃən kəntroʊl/

VEHICLE COMPONENTS: BODYWORK, CONTROLS, AND ACCESSORIES

NOUN **Traction control** is a system that stops the wheels of a vehicle from spinning when excess power is applied.

○ If the rear does begin to skid on a greasy surface, or with too much throttle, traction control takes over.

○ Traction control provides much-needed safety if road conditions cause any of a car's wheels to slip.

trac|tor¹ /træktər/ (short for **tractor unit**) (**tractors**)

VEHICLE TYPES

NOUN A **tractor** is a short vehicle with a powerful engine and a driver's cab. It is used to pull a trailer, such as in a tractor-trailer.

○ The truck was an 18-wheeler with a white tractor.

○ The warehouse attached the semitrailer to the fifth wheel of the tractor unit.

trac|tor² /træktər/ (**tractors**)

VEHICLE TYPES

NOUN A **tractor** is a farm vehicle that is used to pull farm machinery.

○ He has a license to drive an agricultural tractor.

○ Companies that manufacture higher horsepower tractors (greater than 40-hp) have been constrained to import the engines and components because no domestic manufacturer made them.

trail|er /ˈtreɪlər/ (**trailers**)

VEHICLE TYPES

NOUN A **trailer** is a container on wheels which is pulled by a vehicle and which is used for transporting large or heavy items.

○ *The trailer is connected to the tractor by means of a kingpin.*

○ *The truck's engine is a powerhouse for pulling boats, horse boxes, and trailers.*

trail|ing arm /ˈtreɪlɪŋ ɑrm/ (**trailing arms**)

VEHICLE COMPONENTS: BRAKES, STEERING, WHEELS, TIRES, AND SUSPENSION

NOUN A **trailing arm** is part of the suspension for the axle of a vehicle which moves up and down as the vehicle travels over a bumpy surface.

○ *The car had trailing arm front suspension.*

○ *You can adjust the angle of the trailing arm to fine-tune the amount of rear steer.*

trans|fer box (In BRIT use **transfer gearbox**) /ˈtrænsfər bɒks/ (**transfer boxes**)

VEHICLE COMPONENTS: ENGINE, TRANSMISSION, AND EXHAUST

NOUN A **transfer box** is a gear system that divides the power between the front and rear axles of a four-wheel drive system.

○ *The reverse gear is housed in the transfer box in the rear axle unit.*

○ *The rear axle is driven directly from the transfer box via propeller shafts.*

trans|mis|sion[1] /trænzˈmɪʃən/

VEHICLE COMPONENTS: ENGINE, TRANSMISSION, AND EXHAUST

NOUN **Transmission** is the mechanical unit containing a manual or automatic gear system and its operating machinery.

○ *The car was fitted with automatic transmission.*

○ *His car has a four-speed floor-mounted transmission with overdrive and also power steering.*

trans|mis|sion² /trænzmɪʃⁿn/

VEHICLE COMPONENTS: ENGINE, TRANSMISSION, AND EXHAUST

NOUN **Transmission** refers to all the parts, such as the clutch, gearbox, and drive shaft, that transfer the engine power of a vehicle to the wheels.

○ This model has the engine at the front of the car and the transmission at the rear.

○ A flexible cable connects the transmission driveshaft which drives the wheels.

trans|mis|sion brake /trænzmɪʃⁿn breɪk/ (**transmission brakes**)

VEHICLE COMPONENTS: BRAKES, STEERING, WHEELS, TIRES, AND SUSPENSION

NOUN A **transmission brake** is a brake that operates on the transmission system of a vehicle rather than directly on the wheels.

○ When four wheel brakes were fitted, the transmission brake was gradually phased out.

○ The transmission brake of a shaft driven car is applied to a drum carried by the driving shaft.

tread (In BRIT use **track**) /trɛd/

DESIGN AND PERFORMANCE

NOUN **Tread** in a vehicle is the distance between the left and right side wheels on the same axle.

○ The wheel house openings of the car body were big enough to accommodate this tread increase without body changes.

○ Tread width on the front axle was adjustable from 48 to 80 inches.

▶ COLLOCATIONS:
tread depth
tread width

trip com|put|er /trɪp kəmpyutər/ (**trip computers**)

VEHICLE COMPONENTS: LIGHTING AND ELECTRICAL/ELECTRONIC SYSTEMS

NOUN A **trip computer** in a vehicle gives readings of average speed, fuel consumption, and fuel cost per mile.

○ *Like the other versions, they have a trip computer with pre-set speed warning as standard.*

○ *According to the trip computer on my car, it is easy to beat 50mpg on a steady drive on the open road.*

---

truck /trʌk/ (**trucks**)

VEHICLE TYPES

NOUN A **truck** is a large vehicle that is used to transport goods by road.

○ *Large trucks weigh between 5 and 30 tonnes.*

○ *There were delays on the highway after a heavy truck shed its load.*

---

trunk /trʌŋk/ (**trunks**)

VEHICLE COMPONENTS: BODYWORK, CONTROLS, AND ACCESSORIES

NOUN The **trunk** of a car is a covered space at the back or front in which you put luggage or other things.

○ *She put the luggage in the trunk of the car.*

○ *Trunk space is generous and the fold-down rear seats provide additional cargo capacity.*

▶ COLLOCATIONS:
  open the trunk
  shut the trunk

---

tune¹ /tun/ (**tunes**)

DESIGN AND PERFORMANCE

NOUN The **tune** of an engine is how well it is operating.

○ *Below 3600 rpm, the engine goes back to its original state of tune, which means it uses less fuel.*

○ *The more efficient engine tune has also improved the fuel consumption.*

▶ COLLOCATION:
  in tune

t

tune² /tun/ (**tunes, tuned, tuning**)

DESIGN AND PERFORMANCE

VERB When the engine of a vehicle **is tuned**, it is adjusted so that it works well.

○ *The engine was rebuilt and carefully tuned by engineers.*

○ *The engine is tuned to produce around 75 brake horsepower.*

---

tur|bo|charg|er (ABBR **turbo**) /tɜrboʊtʃɑrdʒər/ (**turbochargers**)

VEHICLE COMPONENTS: ENGINE, TRANSMISSION, AND EXHAUST

NOUN A **turbocharger** raises the pressure of the air or air/fuel mixture in an engine with a turbine that uses the energy in the engine's exhaust gases to drive a compressor.

○ *A new turbocharger and intercooler were installed to boost the performance.*

○ *The engine pulls the vehicle's bulk with ease once the turbocharger has puffed itself up to speed.*

---

turn|ing cir|cle /tɜrnɪŋ sɜrkəl/ (**turning circles**)

DESIGN AND PERFORMANCE

NOUN A **turning circle** is the radius of the circle about which a vehicle turns when steered.

○ *Its compact dimensions, excellent turning circle, and effortless handling combine to give exceptional maneuverability.*

○ *The car's turning circle is tiny, making it easy to park.*

---

turn sig|nal (In BRIT use **indicator**) /tɜn sɪgnəl/ (**turn signals**)

VEHICLE COMPONENTS: BODYWORK, CONTROLS, AND ACCESSORIES

NOUN A vehicle's **turn signals** are the flashing lights that tell you that it is going to turn left or right.

○ *All vehicles have high-mounted brake lights and turn signals.*

○ *New wraparound turn signals and clear headlamps give the car a sporty feel.*

twin cam|shaft /twɪn kæmʃæft/ (**twin camshafts**)

VEHICLE COMPONENTS: ENGINE, TRANSMISSION, AND EXHAUST

NOUN A **twin camshaft** is an arrangement of two parallel camshafts for each set of cylinders in an engine. Usually one operates the intake valve and the other the exhaust valve.

○ *The belt drive for a horizontally opposed twin camshaft engine consists of two separate belt drives.*

○ *Most twin camshaft engines have camshafts that are chain-driven or belt-driven.*

twist grip /twɪst grɪp/ (**twist grips**)

VEHICLE COMPONENTS: BODYWORK, CONTROLS, AND ACCESSORIES

NOUN A **twist grip** is a control that you operate by twisting it with your hand, such as the control for the throttle of a motorcycle.

○ *Disconnect the throttle cable at the twist grip.*

○ *The throttle is a twist grip that the rider turns to increase speed.*

two-stroke cy|cle /tu stroʊk saɪkᵊl/

VEHICLE COMPONENTS: ENGINE, TRANSMISSION, AND EXHAUST

NOUN A **two-stroke cycle** is the cycle of engine operation in which the induction, compression, ignition, and exhaust stroke take place within one revolution of the engine.

○ *In theory, the two-stroke cycle diesel engine should develop twice as much power as a four-stroke cycle engine.*

○ *Two-stroke cycle gasoline engines are mainly used in scooters, motorcycles, and three-wheelers.*

RELATED WORDS

Compare **two-stroke cycle** with the **four-stroke cycle** which requires four strokes of the piston: for induction, compression, ignition, and exhaust.

Uu

un|der|bod|y /ˌʌndərbɒdi/ (**underbodies**)

NOUN The **underbody** is the body structure of the underside of a vehicle.

○ *Several areas of the chassis and underbody had to be cleaned and repainted.*

○ *Different body styles can be bolted on to the underbody containing the fuel cell.*

un|der|steer /ˌʌndərstɪər/

NOUN **Understeer** is the tendency of a vehicle to turn less sharply than expected.

○ *By increasing front tire pressures, you can decrease understeer.*

○ *Understeer is when the car tends to carry on straight ahead rather than turning into the corner as sharply as you would wish.*

u|ni|ver|sal joint (ABBR **UJ**) /ˌyuːnɪvɜrsᵊl dʒɔɪnt/ (**universal joints**)

NOUN A **universal joint** is a type of joint that connects two rotating shafts, allowing them to move in all directions.

○ *When they took the rear driveshaft out, they discovered a seized universal joint.*

○ *The transmission output shaft fed directly into the differential, with just one universal joint in between.*

Vv

---

vac|u|um brake /væzkyum breɪk/ (**vacuum brakes**)

VEHICLE COMPONENTS: BRAKES, STEERING, WHEELS, TIRES, AND SUSPENSION

NOUN A **vacuum brake** is a type of brake that works by atmospheric pressure acting on a piston in a vacuum cylinder.

- ○ *Vacuum brake equipment has been replaced with modern air brake equipment.*
- ○ *A vacuum brake system is operated by a vacuum taken from the intake manifold or carburetor at a point just above the throttle valve.*

---

vac|u|um ser|vo /væzkyum sɜrvoʊ/ (**vacuum servos**)

VEHICLE COMPONENTS: BODYWORK, CONTROLS, AND ACCESSORIES

NOUN A **vacuum servo** is a servo-mechanism using atmospheric pressure acting on a piston in a vacuum cylinder to operate a system such as a brake.

- ○ *To adjust the speed, the vacuum servo controls the position of the throttle.*
- ○ *The vacuum servo is mounted between the brake pedal and the master cylinder.*

---

valve /væzlv/ (**valves**)

VEHICLE COMPONENTS: BODYWORK, CONTROLS, AND ACCESSORIES

NOUN A **valve** is a device attached to a pipe or a tube that controls the flow of air or liquid through the pipe or tube.

- ○ *The specification also includes twin overhead camshafts and four valves per cylinder.*
- ○ *One camshaft operates the intake valve and the other the exhaust valve.*

v

valve bounce /vælv baʊns/ (**valve bounces**)

VEHICLE COMPONENTS: ENGINE, TRANSMISSION, AND EXHAUST

NOUN A **valve bounce** is the bouncing of a poppet valve on its seat when it is closing.

○ *Valve bounce can occur if the valve spring is weak and operated at high speeds.*

○ *Valve bounce is when the valve hits its seat and then bounces back off of it.*

valve lift /vælv lɪft/

VEHICLE COMPONENTS: ENGINE, TRANSMISSION, AND EXHAUST

NOUN The **valve lift** is the distance by which the valve is raised from its seated position when it is fully opened.

○ *These valve springs will allow a maximum safe valve lift of 9.9mm only.*

○ *The camshaft controls the speed of valve opening, valve lift off the valve seat, and how long the valve stays open.*

valve seat /vælv sit/ (**valve seats**)

VEHICLE COMPONENTS: ENGINE, TRANSMISSION, AND EXHAUST

NOUN The **valve seat** is the ring-shaped surface with which a poppet valve closes.

○ *A valve seat is the part of the cylinder head that mates with the valve face.*

○ *Valve seat recession occurs when valve seats wear and the valve sink recedes into the cylinder head.*

valve spring /vælv sprɪŋ/ (**valve springs**)

VEHICLE COMPONENTS: ENGINE, TRANSMISSION, AND EXHAUST

NOUN A **valve spring** is a spring that returns a poppet valve to its closed position.

○ *The valve spring is a coil spring used to hold the valve in a closed position.*

○ *The valve spring must be strong enough to keep the lifter in contact with the camshaft lobe at all times.*

valve tim|ing /vælv taɪmɪŋ/

DESIGN AND PERFORMANCE

NOUN **Valve timing** is the exact timing of the opening and closing of the valves in a piston engine.

○ Carmakers have devised ways to change valve timing while the engine is running.

○ Variable valve timing offers the possibility of controlling the cylinder filling process solely by means of restricting the opening of the inlet valve.

valve train /vælv treɪn/ (**valve trains**)

VEHICLE COMPONENTS: ENGINE, TRANSMISSION, AND EXHAUST

NOUN A **valve train** is the total mechanism that causes the valves of an engine to lift and close.

○ The gasoline additive cleans the valve train so that the intake valves don't stick.

○ The valve train includes the parts that open and close the valves.

van /væn/ (**vans**)

VEHICLE TYPES

NOUN A **van** is a small or medium-sized road vehicle with one row of seats at the front and a space for carrying goods behind.

○ The company's new model of van has a payload of 2000lb.

○ He drives a small delivery van for a local store.

V-belt /viː bɛlt/ (**V-belts**)

VEHICLE COMPONENTS: ENGINE, TRANSMISSION, AND EXHAUST

NOUN A **V-belt** is a rubber belt used for driving mechanisms in an engine such as the fans or water pump.

○ A V-belt must be the right size, extending slightly out of the pulley groove.

○ The V-belt has driven mechanical parts of car engines since the 1920s.

V

ven|ti|la|tion /vɛntᵊleɪʃən/

VEHICLE COMPONENTS: BODYWORK, CONTROLS, AND ACCESSORIES

NOUN   **Ventilation** is a system that provides a draft of air into and out of a vehicle passenger compartment.

○ The car's ventilation system demists the windscreen more quickly when you turn on the air cooling.

○ The only ventilation comes from quarterlights and tiny sliding windows in the doors, all the rear windows being fixed.

Ven|tu|ri /vɛntʊəri/ (**Venturis**)

VEHICLE COMPONENTS: ENGINE, TRANSMISSION, AND EXHAUST

NOUN   In a vehicle, a **Venturi** is a nozzle which accelerates and lowers static pressure in gases or vapors flowing through it. Named after Italian physicist Giovanni Venturi.

○ If the Venturi is too large, the flow of air is slow and will not atomize sufficient fuel to make a balanced mixture.

○ In the days before fuel-injection, the "Venturi" was a feature of carburetors. Without it fuel couldn't be drawn from the tank to mix with the flow of air.

vol|u|met|ric ef|fi|cien|cy /vɒlyəmɛtrɪk ɪfɪʃᵊnsi/

DESIGN AND PERFORMANCE

NOUN   The **volumetric efficiency** of an engine is the extent to which the cylinder is completely filled by the air/fuel mixture that enters on each exhaust stroke. This measures the ability of an engine to breathe freely.

○ The easier the engine breathes, the greater its volumetric efficiency, and the more power it produces.

○ The volumetric efficiency of an engine can be reduced by restricting the airflow in and out of the engine.

V

Ww

---

warm up /wɔrm ʌp/ (warms up, warmed up, warming up)

DESIGN AND PERFORMANCE

VERB If an engine **warms up**, it reaches the right running temperature and becomes ready for use a little while after being switched on.

○ *The sound goes away within seconds as the engine warms up.*

○ *Modern engines don't need a lot of time to warm up.*

---

wheel /wil/ (wheels)

VEHICLE COMPONENTS: BRAKES, STEERING, WHEELS, TIRES, AND SUSPENSION

NOUN The **wheels** of a vehicle are the circular objects that are attached underneath it and that enable it to move along the ground.

○ *The car wheels spun and slipped on some oil on the road.*

○ *The coupe has 17-inch tires on aluminum six-spoke wheels.*

> **WHEEL PARTS INCLUDE:**
>
> hub, hubcap, kingpin, rim, wheel nut
>
> The space in a vehicle's structure where the wheel is positioned is a **wheel well** and the part of the car's body above it is the **wheel arch**.

---

wheel arch /wil artʃ/ (wheel arches)

VEHICLE COMPONENTS: BODYWORK, CONTROLS, AND ACCESSORIES

NOUN The **wheel arch** is the semicircular part positioned above the wheel of a vehicle.

○ The most important body change was that the front wheel arch was cut higher into the fender.

○ Corrosion had occurred around the splash plate at the back of the wheel arch.

---

wheel|base /wiːlbeɪs/ (**wheelbases**)

DESIGN AND PERFORMANCE

NOUN The **wheelbase** of a vehicle is the distance between its front and back wheels.

○ The longer wheelbase combined with much firmer suspension really inspires confidence.

○ Crosswinds are a danger for a car that rides tall on a short wheelbase.

---

wheel nut /wiːl nʌt/ (**wheel nuts**)

VEHICLE COMPONENTS: BRAKES, STEERING, WHEELS, TIRES, AND SUSPENSION

NOUN A **wheel nut** is a nut which attaches the wheel of a vehicle to its hub.

○ To remove the hub, use the wrench to slacken each wheel nut by one turn.

○ Make sure you tighten the wheel nuts after changing the tire.

---

wheel well /wiːl wɛl/ (**wheel wells**)

VEHICLE COMPONENTS: BODYWORK, CONTROLS, AND ACCESSORIES

NOUN A **wheel well** is the space in a vehicle's structure where the wheel is positioned.

○ The offset determines how the wheel and tire are centered in the wheel well.

○ When you look at your suspension, first look at it with the wheel facing forward to see if the wheel is making contact with the wheel well.

---

wind|shield /wɪndʃiːld/ (**windshields**)

VEHICLE COMPONENTS: BODYWORK, CONTROLS, AND ACCESSORIES

NOUN The **windshield** of a vehicle is the glass window at the front through which the driver looks.

○ The front windshield of the car was smashed by the impact.

○ The image of the road ahead is projected onto the lower part of the windshield.

US/UK ENGLISH

Windshield is one of the many vehicle parts that has a different name in British English, where it is called a **windscreen**. Other differences include the following:
hood US, **bonnet** UK
license plate US, **number plate** UK
fender US, **wing** UK
antenna US, **aerial** UK
trunk US, **boot** UK
turn signal US, **indicator** UK

---

wind|shield wip|er /wɪndʃild waɪpər/ (**windshield wipers**)

VEHICLE COMPONENTS: BODYWORK, CONTROLS, AND ACCESSORIES

NOUN A **windshield wiper** is a device that wipes rain from a vehicle's windshield.

○ *Even with the car's windshield wipers going at full speed, I was barely able to see ahead of me.*

○ *I had to keep the windshield wipers on fast speed as the rain continued to fall heavily.*

---

wip|er blade /waɪpər bleɪd/ (**wiper blades**)

VEHICLE COMPONENTS: BODYWORK, CONTROLS, AND ACCESSORIES

NOUN A **wiper blade** is the blade of a windshield wiper.

○ *Temperature extremes on the windshield have a damaging effect on wiper blade performance.*

○ *Install new wiper blades at least once a year to ensure good vision.*

---

wir|ing har|ness /waɪərɪŋ hɑrnɪs/ (**wiring harnesses**)

VEHICLE COMPONENTS: LIGHTING AND ELECTRICAL/ELECTRONIC SYSTEMS

NOUN A **wiring harness** is the complete electrical wiring system of a vehicle.

○ *Once the chassis structure is assembled, the wiring harness, brake and fuel lines are put in place.*

○ *An extensive network of wires form the wiring harness of a car.*

w

Zz

zinc /zɪŋk/

NOUN **Zinc** is a bluish-white metal which is used to make other metals, or to cover other metals, such as steel, as a protective coating.

○ *Zinc is a common environmental contaminant, because it is sprayed on cars to prevent rust.*

○ *The galvanized finish is coated with zinc to stop it from rusting.*

> **METALS AND METALLIC ELEMENTS USED IN CAR MANUFACTURE**
>
> aluminum, chromium, nickel, stainless steel, steel, zinc

Practice and Solutions

1. Choose the correct phrase to fill each gap.

1 .... is a panel that separates the engine compartment from the passenger compartment of a vehicle.
a A D-post   **b** A bulkhead   **c** An underbody

2 .... is the main shaft of an internal combustion engine.
a A half-shaft   **b** A torsion bar   **c** A crankshaft

3 .... is a small area, usually in the cylinder head, in which combustion is started before fuel enters into the main combustion chamber.
a A manifold   **b** A transfer box   **c** A prechamber

4 .... is the part of an engine gear train that converts the cam lift into linear reciprocating movement, which it transmits to the valve.
a A tappet   **b** A crank   **c** A gasket

5 .... is a device for reducing vibration in an engine, camshaft drive, or vehicle suspension.
a A snubber   **b** A damper   **c** A governor

6 .... is the part of an engine in which air and fuel are mixed together to form a vapor that can be burned.
a A carburetor   **b** An alternator   **c** A piston land

2. Find the words or phrases that do not belong.

1 Engines ....
a oversquare engine   **b** reciprocating engine   **c** replying engine
d spark ignition engine

2 Ratios ....
a crank-drive ratio   **b** air-fuel ratio   **c** bore-stroke ratio
d compression ratio

3 Shafts ....
   a cardan shaft   **b** oversquare shaft   **c** layshaft   **d** drive shaft

4 Strokes ....
   a compression stroke   **b** firing stroke   **c** V-stroke   **d** induction stroke

5 Plugs ....
   a drain plug   **b** glow plug   **c** spark plug   **d** aspirating plug

6 Belts ....
   a fan belt   **b** V-belt   **c** poppet belt   **d** timing belt

3. Which sentences are correct?

1 An alternator creates an electrical current that changes direction as it flows.   ....

2 A distributor is filled with water in order to cool the engine.   ....

3 An injector introduces fuel under pressure into the combustion system of an engine.   ....

4 A carburetor is an engine-driven switch that sends the high-voltage ignition current to each spark plug in turn.   ....

5 An accelerator shows engine cylinder pressure during a working cycle.   ....

6 A governor limits the maximum speed of an engine, especially a diesel engine.   ....

4. Rearrange the letters to find words. Use the definitions to help you.

1 **ydobkrow** ....
(the outside part of a vehicle)

2 **drbshadoa** ....
(the panel facing the driver's seat where most of the instruments and switches are)

3 **tinareefze** ....
(a liquid that is added to the cooling water of an engine to stop it from freezing in cold weather)

4 **eknadrabh** ....
(a brake that the driver operates with his or her hand)

5 **krntu** ....
(a covered space at the back or front of a vehicle in which you put luggage or other things)

6 **ligetata** ....
(a door at the back of a vehicle that is hinged at the bottom so that it opens downward)

7 **ermemodo** ....
(a device in a vehicle which shows how far the vehicle has traveled)

8 **chatackbh** ....
(a car with an extra door at the back that opens upward)

5. Put the correct word in each gap.

fascia	guttering	jack	chassis	stick shift	choke

1 .... the framework that a vehicle is built on

2 .... a device for lifting a vehicle off the ground

3 .... the part surrounding the instruments and dials

4 .... the lever that you use to change gear in a vehicle

5 .... a device that reduces the amount of air going into the engine and makes it easier to start the engine or run it in cold weather

6 .... the curved edge at the side of the roof panel of a vehicle, along which rain water is channeled away

6. Put each sentence into the correct order.

1 an additional / for the journey / we took / across the desert / spare wheel

....

....

2 most of / of the caravan / over the drawbar / the weight / should be

....

....

3 saved him / injury when / from serious / he crashed his car / the air bag

....

....

4 at full speed / through the rain / with his windshield / Peter drove / wipers going

....

....

5 a patch of ice / into a tree / her car / and crashed / skidded on

....

....

6 may have / motors with a / a separate / turbocharger / oil filter

....

....

7. For each question, choose the correct answer.

1 A flat shape such as a wing that is intended to produce a particular effect from the flow of air is ....
   a a fender   **b** an airfoil   **c** a fairing

2 A centrally pivoted lever in the valve train of an engine that converts the motion of the rods to open the valves is ....
   a a track rod   **b** a torsion bar   **c** a rocker arm

3 A type of joint that connects two rotating shafts, allowing them to move in all directions is ....
   a a wheel nut   **b** a universal joint   **c** a filter

4 A type of transmission in which all forward gear pairs remain engaged is ....
   a a constant mesh gearbox   **b** a reciprocating engine
   c a planetary transmission

5 The end of a connecting rod that engages with a crankshaft is
   ....
   a a big end   **b** an end float   **c** a terminal post

6 A shaft bearing in which a shaft rotates lubricated by oil or grease is
   ....
   a a needle valve   **b** a rich mixture   **c** a plain bearing

8. Choose the correct word or phrase to fill each gap.

quench   purge   bleed

1 If you .... a fluid from a container or system, you drain and remove all traces of it.

skids   overheats   stalls

2 If a vehicle ...., the engine stops suddenly.

tune   bleed   stall

3 If you .... a fuel system, you empty it of fluid in order to work on it or refill it with fresh fluid.

revs up   ticks over   jackknifes

4 If a truck that is in two parts ...., the back part swings around at a sharp angle to the front part in an uncontrolled way.

backfires	backs up	purges

5 When a vehicle or its engine ...., it produces an explosion in the exhaust pipe.

stalling	tuning	ticking over

6 If an engine is .... it is running at a low speed without moving.

9. Match the two parts together.

1 The purpose of an immobilizer

2 The purpose of a supercharger

3 The purpose of a damper

4 The purpose of a circuit breaker

5 The purpose of a muffler

6 The purpose of a catalytic converter

a is to make the exhaust quieter.

b is to reduce the pollution coming from a car's exhaust.

c is to stop people from stealing your car.

d is to reduce the vibration, for example in an engine.

e is to stop the flow of electricity if something goes wrong.

f is to increase the pressure of air and gases that are drawn into an engine.

10. For each question, choose the correct answer.

1 The extent to which the cylinder is completely filled by the air/fuel mixture that enters on each exhaust stroke is known as ....
a spring rate   b volumetric efficiency   c capacity

2 The study of how equipment and parts in a vehicle can be arranged in the most efficient and comfortable way is called ....

a emissions analysis   b capacity   c ergonomics

3 The radius of the circle within which a vehicle turns when steered is its
   ....
   a turn signal   b turning circle   c clearance volume

4 The amount of liquid a container such as a fuel tank can hold is its
   ....
   a capacity   b compression   c displacement

5 The grip that the wheels of a vehicle have on the ground is ....
   a compression   b handling   c traction

6 A piece of machinery on which the wheels of a vehicle can ride in order
   to test how well the vehicle works under road conditions is a ....
   a chassis dynamometer   b bench seat   c rolling road

11. Choose the correct phrase to fill each gap.

A header tank   A fuel tank   An intake manifold

1 .... is a container of liquid positioned at a
   higher level than a main tank, so that the level of pressure can be
   maintained.

A kingpin   A snubber   A filter

2 .... is a rubber or metal spring device on a
   vehicle that limits the movement of a mechanism.

An antenna   An air foil   A connecting rod

3 .... is a device or a piece of wire that sends
   and receives radio signals.

A torsion bar	A crankpin	A fuel rail

4 .... is the part of the crank of a crankshaft to which the connecting rod is attached.

An injection pump	A cylinder head	A header tank

5 .... is a device that supplies fuel under pressure to the injector of a fuel injection system.

An intercooler	A brake servo	A supercharger

6 .... is a mechanical pump or compressor for increasing the pressure of air or gases that are drawn into an engine.

12. Complete the sentences by writing one word or phrase in each gap.

trip computer	tailgate	retreaded tires
underbody	antifreeze	handbrake

1 There is a lot of rust on the .... of the vehicle.

2 Make sure you put plenty of .... in the water.

3 When you come to a stop, put the .... on.

4 He let down the .... so the dog could jump out.

5 According to the ...., we've averaged 55 miles per hour.

6 I bought .... because they are cheaper than new ones.

13. Find the words or phrases that do not belong.

1 Things connected with the suspension ....
 a A-arm **b** carcass **c** torsion bar **d** MacPherson strut

2 Things connected with the brakes ....
 a muffler **b** caliper **c** electric retarder **d** diaphragm

3 Things connected with the exhaust ....
 a particulate filter **b** muffler **c** turbocharger **d** layshaft

4 Things connected with the gears and gearbox ....
 a balk ring **b** caliper **c** layshaft **d** differential

5 Things connected with the tires ....
 a carcass **b** blowout **c** diaphragm **d** inner tube

6 Things connected with the wheels ....
 a lock **b** D-post **c** hubcap **d** axle

14. Match the two parts together.

1 ABS is	**a** the point at which the piston of an engine is nearest to the axis of a crankshaft.
2 LPG is	**b** the study of the noise and vibration levels of vehicles.
3 BDC is	**c** an alternative type of fuel for vehicles.
4 BHP is	**d** the amount of fuel consumed by a vehicle for each unit of power output.
5 NVH is	**e** a measure of engine power.
6 SFC is	**f** a system that stops the wheels from locking when you brake.

PRACTICE PRACTICE PRACTICE PRACTICE PRACTICE

15. Complete the sentences by writing one word or phrase in each gap.

| Low-profile | normally aspirated | eccentric |
| horizontally-opposed | anti-knock | Ergonomic |

1 An .... agent helps to make an engine function more smoothly.

2 .... tires have a wide tread and a thin sidewall.

3 .... equipment or parts in a vehicle are designed to be comfortable or efficient for a passenger or driver.

4 An .... component of a vehicle rotates around an off-center axis.

5 A .... engine has the cylinders set horizontally at either side of the crankshaft.

6 A .... engine breathes air at atmospheric pressure.

16. Rearrange the letters to find words. Use the definitions to help you.

1 **tssnoiimrsna** ....
(the mechanical unit containing a manual or automatic gear system and its operating machinery)

2 **ssniousnep** ....
(the springs and other devices attached to the wheels of a vehicle that give a smooth ride over uneven ground)

3 **rgonaiddhlo** ....
(how well a vehicle responds to being driven and how easy it is to control)

4 **everdrovi** ....
(a very high gear that is used when you are driving at high speeds)

5 **esterrevo** ....
(the tendency of a vehicle to turn more sharply than expected)

6 **lenratu** ....
(the position between the gears of a vehicle, in which the gears are not connected to the engine)

7 **dlamofin** ....
(a system of pipes that divides a flow and carries it to more than one place or that brings a flow from a number of places to a single place)

8 **kkonc** ....
(the noise caused by part of the air-fuel mixture in an engine cylinder burning before the normal combustion started by a spark)

PRACTICE PRACTICE PRACTICE PRACTICE PRACTICE

17. Put the correct word in each gap.

| off-highway vehicle | automatic | semitrailer |
| convertible | hatchback | hybrid vehicle |

1 .... a car with a soft roof that can be folded down or removed

2 .... a vehicle using two different forms of power, such as an electric motor and an internal combustion engine, or an electric motor with a battery and fuel cells for energy storage

3 .... a vehicle with automatic transmission

4 .... a vehicle, such as one used for construction or agriculture, that is intended for use on steep or uneven ground

5 .... the long rear section of a truck that can bend when it turns

6 .... a car with an extra door at the back that opens upward

18. Which sentences are correct?

1 Carbon monoxide is a harmless gas that is produced especially by the engines of vehicles. ....

2 A lean mixture is a fuel/air mixture containing a relatively high proportion of fuel. ....

3 Multigrade oil is engine or gear oil that works well at
both low and high temperatures. ....

4 The octane number of a fuel, especially gasoline, is
a measure of the energy it produces. ....

5 LPG consists of hydrocarbon gases in solid form. ....

6 Cetane is a colorless liquid hydrocarbon found
in petroleum. ....

19. Complete the sentences by writing one word or phrase in each gap.

camber	indicator	handling
bench test	wheelbase	spring rate

1 A .... is an operating test carried out on an
engine or other major part removed from a vehicle.

2 The .... of a vehicle is how well it responds to
being driven and how easy it is to control.

3 The .... is a measurement of the amount of
force needed to compress a spring a particular distance.

4 A .... is a gradual downward slope from the
center of a road to each side of it.

5 An .... is an instrument that shows engine
cylinder pressure during a working cycle.

6 The .... of a vehicle is the distance between its
front and back wheels.

20. Put each sentence into the correct order.

1 catching up with us / rearview mirror that / see in the / I could
/ his car was

....

....

2 heavy trucks and / about 15% / semitrailers make up / on the highway
/ of all traffic

....

....

3 will be recycled / for use / in cars / into biodiesel / the fat

....

....

4 remote control / and an engine / the car has / central locking
/ immobilizer

....

....

5 he drove / fan belt / produced a / the loose / screeching noise as

....

....

6 to write down / license plate before / she drove away / I was able
/ the number of the

....

....

Solutions

Exercise 1
1   b   A bulkhead
2   c   A crankshaft
3   c   A prechamber
4   a   A tappet
5   b   A damper
6   a   A carburetor

Exercise 2
1   c   replying engine
2   a   crank-drive ratio
3   b   oversquare shaft
4   c   V-stroke
5   d   aspirating plug
6   c   poppet belt

Exercise 3
1   An alternator creates an electrical current that changes direction as it flows.
3   An injector introduces fuel under pressure into the combustion system of an engine.
6   A governor limits the maximum speed of an engine, especially a diesel engine.

Exercise 4
1   bodywork
2   dashboard
3   antifreeze
4   handbrake
5   trunk
6   tailgate
7   odometer
8   hatchback

Exercise 5
1   chassis
2   jack
3   fascia
4   stick shift
5   choke
6   guttering

Exercise 6
1   we took an additional spare wheel for the journey across the desert
2   most of the weight of the caravan should be over the drawbar
3   the air bag saved him from serious injury when he crashed his car
4   Peter drove through the rain with his windshield wipers going at full speed
5   her car skidded on a patch of ice and crashed into a tree
6   motors with a turbocharger may have a separate oil filter

Exercise 7
1   b   an airfoil
2   c   a rocker arm
3   b   a universal joint
4   a   a constant mesh gearbox
5   a   a big end
6   c   a plain bearing

Exercise 8
1   purge
2   stalls
3   bleed
4   jackknifes
5   backfires
6   ticking over

Exercise 9
1   c   is to stop people from stealing your car.
2   f   is to increase the pressure of air and gases that are drawn into an engine.
3   d   is to reduce the vibration, for example in an engine.
4   e   is to stop the flow of electricity if something goes wrong.
5   a   is to make the exhaust quieter.
6   b   is to reduce the pollution coming from a car's exhaust.

Exercise 10
1   b   volumetric efficiency
2   c   ergonomics
3   b   turning circle
4   a   capacity
5   c   traction
6   c   rolling road

Exercise 11
1   A header tank
2   A snubber
3   An antenna
4   A crankpin
5   An injection pump
6   A supercharger

Exercise 12
1   underbody
2   antifreeze
3   handbrake
4   tailgate
5   trip computer
6   retreaded tires

Exercise 13
1   b   carcass
2   a   muffler
3   d   layshaft
4   b   caliper
5   c   diaphragm
6   b   D-post

Exercise 14
1   f   a system that stops the wheels from locking when you brake.
2   c   an alternative type of fuel for vehicles.
3   a   the point at which the piston of an engine is nearest to the axis of a crankshaft.
4   e   a measure of engine power.
5   b   the study of the noise and vibration levels of vehicles.
6   d   the amount of fuel consumed by a vehicle for each unit of power output.

Exercise 15
1   anti-knock
2   Low-profile
3   Ergonomic
4   eccentric
5   horizontally-opposed
6   normally aspirated

Exercise 16
1   transmission
2   suspension
3   roadholding
4   overdrive
5   oversteer
6   neutral
7   manifold
8   knock

Exercise 17
1   convertible
2   hybrid vehicle
3   automatic
4   off-highway vehicle
5   semitrailer
6   hatchback

Exercise 18
3   Multigrade oil is engine or gear oil that works well at both low and high temperatures.
5   LPG consists of hydrocarbon gases in solid form.
6   Cetane is a colorless liquid hydrocarbon found in petroleum.

Exercise 19
1   bench test
2   handling
3   spring rate
4   camber
5   indicator
6   wheelbase

Exercise 20
1   I could see in the rearview mirror that his car was catching up with us
2   heavy trucks and semitrailers make up about 15% of all traffic on the highway
3   the fat will be recycled into biodiesel for use in cars
4   the car has remote control central locking and an engine immobilizer
5   the loose fan belt produced a screeching noise as he drove
6   I was able to write down the number of the license plate before she drove away

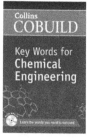

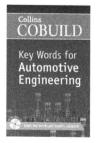

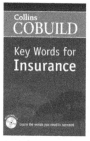

www.ingramcontent.com/pod-product-compliance
Ingram Content Group UK Ltd.
Pitfield, Milton Keynes, MK11 3LW, UK
UKHW021618180325
456415UK00005B/12